*Great Meals in Minutes* was created by
Rebus, Inc.
and published by Time-Life Books.

**Rebus, Inc.**

*Publisher:* Rodney Friedman
*Editor:* Shirley Tomkievicz
*Executive Editor:* Elizabeth P. Rice
*Art Director:* Ronald Gross
*Senior Editors:* Brenda Goldberg,
Cara De Silva, Ruth A. Peltason
*Food Editor and Food Stylist:* Grace Young
*Photographer:* Steven Mays
*Prop Stylist:* Zazel Wilde Lovén
*Staff Writer:* Alexandra Greeley
*Associate Editor:* Jordan Verner
*Editorial Assistant:* Donna Kalvarsky
*Photography, Styling Assistant:* Cathryn
Schwing
*Editorial Board:* Angelica Cannon, Sally
Dorst, Lilyan Glusker, Kim MacArthur,
Valerie Marchant, Joan Whitman

For information about any Time-Life book,
please write:
Reader Information
Time-Life Books
541 North Fairbanks Court
Chicago, Illinois 60611

Library of Congress Cataloging in Publication Data
Brunch menus.
    (Great meals in minutes)
    Includes index.
    1. Brunches.   2. Menus   3. Cooks—
United States— Biography.
I. Time-Life Books.   II. Series.
TX733.B75   1984    642    83-24172
ISBN 0-86706-171-5 (lib. bdg.)
ISBN 0-86706-170-7 (retail ed.)

Time-Life Books Inc.
is a wholly owned subsidiary of
**Time Incorporated**

*Founder:* Henry R. Luce 1898–1967

*Editor-in-Chief:* Henry Anatole Grunwald
*President:* J. Richard Munro
*Chairman of the Board:* Ralph P. Davidson
*Executive Vice President:* Clifford J. Grum
*Editorial Director:* Ralph Graves
*Group Vice President, Books:* Joan D. Manley

**Time-Life Books Inc.**

*Editor:* George Constable
*Executive Editor:* George Daniels
*Director of Design:* Louis Klein
*Board of Editors:* Dale M. Brown, Thomas A.
Lewis, Robert G. Mason, Ellen Phillips,
Gerry Schremp, Gerald Simons, Rosalind
Stubenberg, Kit van Tulleken
*Director of Administration:* David L. Harrison
*Director of Research:* Carolyn L. Sackett
*Director of Photography:* John Conrad Weiser

*President:* Reginald K. Brack Jr.
*Senior Vice President:* William Henry
*Vice Presidents:* George Artandi, Stephen L.
Bair, Peter G. Barnes, Robert A. Ellis,
Juanita T. James, Christopher T. Linen,
James L. Mercer, Joanne A. Pello,
Paul R. Stewart

*Editorial Operations*
*Design:* Anne B. Landry (art coordinator);
James J. Cox (quality control)
*Research:* Phyllis K. Wise (assistant director),
Louise D. Forstall
*Copy Room:* Diane Ullius (director),
Celia Beattie
*Production:* Gordon E. Buck,
Peter Inchauteguiz
*Correspondent:* Miriam Hsia (New York)

SERIES CONSULTANT
Margaret E. Happel is the author of *Ladies
Home Journal Adventures in Cooking,
Ladies Home Journal Handbook of Holiday
Cuisine,* and other best-selling cookbooks, as
well as the translator and adapter of Rebecca
Hsu Hiu Min's *Delights of Chinese Cooking.*
A food consultant based in New York City,
she has been director of the food department
of *Good Housekeeping* and editor of
*American Home* magazine.

WINE CONSULTANT
Tom Maresca combines a full-time career
teaching English literature with writing
about and consuming fine wines. He is the
author of *Mastering Wine a Taste at a Time.*

*Cover:* Diane Darrow and Tom Maresca's
smoked sable and salmon rolls with cream
cheese and caviar, chicken breasts Béarnaise,
and broiled peach halves with raspberry jam.
See pages 55–57.

# Great Meals
IN MINUTES

# BRUNCH
# MENUS

TIME-LIFE BOOKS, ALEXANDRIA, VIRGINIA

# Contents

# Meet the Cooks

### MARGARET FOX

Margaret Fox is a pastry chef turned restaurateur. In 1977, she opened "Café Beaujolais" in Mendocino, California. From 1977 to 1980, as a staff member of the Great Chefs of France Cooking School in northern California, she was responsible for providing breakfasts for the visiting French chefs who taught there. Now, she cooks for the restaurant, and teaches classes on omelet making and breakfasts.

### RUTH SPEAR

Ruth Spear is a journalist and food writer whose articles about food have appeared in *New York* magazine, *Travel & Leisure*, *Food & Wine*, *Cuisine*, and *Harper's Bazaar.* Currently food editor of *Avenue* magazine, she is also the author of *The East Hampton Cookbook* and *Cooking Fish and Shellfish*. Ruth Spear lives in New York City.

### MARIA ROBBINS

Born in Russia, Maria Polushkin Robbins spent part of her childhood in Germany and then moved to New York. She has written food articles for a Long Island newspaper and is the author of *The Dumpling Cookbook* and the compiler of *The Cook's Quotation Book*. Also a children's book author, she lives in East Hampton, Long Island, with her husband.

### DIANE DARROW AND TOM MARESCA

Diane Darrow and her husband, Tom Maresca, live and work in New York City. They cook—mostly in the Italian manner—as an avocation. Diane Darrow has taught wine appreciation classes, and Tom Maresca is the wine consultant for the *Great Meals in Minutes* series. Together, they have published numerous articles on food, wine, dining, and travel. Each has also pursued a separate career, Diane as an editor and Tom as a teacher.

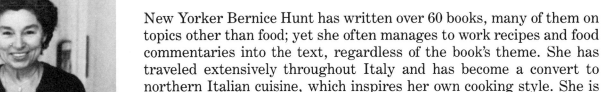

## BERNICE HUNT

New Yorker Bernice Hunt has written over 60 books, many of them on topics other than food; yet she often manages to work recipes and food commentaries into the text, regardless of the book's theme. She has traveled extensively throughout Italy and has become a convert to northern Italian cuisine, which inspires her own cooking style. She is the author of two cookbooks, *Easy Gourmet Cooking* and *Great Bread!*

## CHRISTOPHER STYLER

Christopher Styler is a cum laude graduate of Johnson and Wales College, the Rhode Island college known internationally for its culinary division. After serving as chef at "The Black Dog Tavern" on Martha's Vineyard, he went to the test kitchen of *Food & Wine* magazine. From there, he joined the staff of *Cuisine*. Now, he does free-lance recipe development and works for a restaurant consulting firm in New York City.

## HENRY LEWIS CREEL

A midwesterner by birth, Henry Lewis Creel has lived in New York since 1940. He enjoys preparing simple and delicious meals, trimmed down to small portions so that there will be no leftovers. He used this waste-not principle as the basis of his two cookbooks for single people, *Cooking for One Is Fun* and *Cooking on Your Own*.

## BERT GREENE

For ten years, Bert Greene ran a gourmet take-out shop on Long Island called "The Store." The titles of cookbooks written by him also attest to his love of American cuisine—*The Store Cookbook*, *Bert Greene's Kitchen Bouquets*, and *Honest American Fare*. He writes a weekly food column that appears in the *New York Daily News*, the *Los Angeles Times*, and many other newspapers across the country, and he appears regularly as a guest cook on the television show "Hour Magazine."

## SHELLEY HANDLER

Shelley Handler, who lives in San Francisco, is a graduate of the California Culinary Academy. A professional cook, she has worked as head chef at a two-star restaurant in Milan, Italy, and at "Chez Panisse Café," an innovative restaurant in Berkeley, California. As a cooking instructor, she teaches "The Basics," how to make meals in 15 to 20 minutes. Her recipes have appeared in *The California Artists' Cookbook*.

# Brunch Menus in Minutes

## GREAT MEALS FOR FOUR, IN AN HOUR OR LESS

At its best, brunch is an unhurried meal, an irresistibly comfortable way to entertain family and friends. Because brunch, a merging of breakfast and lunch, is eaten around noontime, cooks can prepare either breakfast or lunch foods, or a combination of both, and serve the meal anytime between midmorning and midafternoon. There are no hard-and-fast rules for brunch, which lends itself to almost any style of entertaining.

Many people assume that brunch is an American invention. But, according to *The Dictionary of American Food & Drink*, Englishman Guy Beringer coined the word in the late nineteenth century, presumably to describe what he ate after a morning's hunt. Sumptuous English hunt breakfasts and lunches probably were the precursors of today's brunch. A proper hunt breakfast was—and still is—a formidable multicourse repast: broths, claret cups, roasts, sweetbreads, fish puddings, herring, aspics, hot breads, egg dishes, fruit tarts, and cakes.

After a tour of the plantation or a gallop to hounds, antebellum southern gentlemen, like their English kin, consumed lavish midmorning meals: sweet pastries, seafood, country hams, eggs, waffles, sweet-potato pies, hominy, vegetables, meats, poultry, tea, and coffee, preceded by jolts of bourbon. To this day, the traditional southern hunt breakfast incorporates much of the same fare.

Other cultures may have influenced the brunch evolution. For centuries, the Chinese have gathered in midmorning for a *dim sum* (literally, "little things that touch the heart") of dumplings, steamed buns, fried rice, tofu, and meat pies served with steaming tea. Austrians pause around ten in the morning for a second "fork" breakfast, or Gabelfrühstück, of goulash or sausages served with spirits. Germany has a similar midmorning custom.

Who cooked the first verifiable American brunch, and where, is a matter of speculation. A New York cook, or one in New Orleans? Whichever was first, the tilt is toward the South. In the mid-1800s, Creole market workers in New Orleans began a late-morning custom of eating a gargantuan second breakfast at Begue's, a coffeehouse. Later, wealthy residents began frequenting Begue's for their late, and leisurely, Sunday breakfasts.

What is probable is that by the mid-1930s brunch had become an American custom, despite Emily Post's disapproval. She wrote in an early edition of her book on American etiquette, "But do not give encouragement to that single-headed, double-bodied deformity of language, brunch. . . . Brunch, breakfast at lunchtime, calls to mind standees at a lunch counter, but *not* the beauty of hospitable living."

On the contrary, today's brunch is the epitome of gracious entertaining. With a leisurely approach and the inclusion of easy-to-prepare foods, brunch becomes the host's response to the hurried pace of modern American life, a time when he or she can shine.

Its flexible format allows varying degrees of informality: besides offering delicious, well-prepared foods, the cook can be creative with imaginative table settings, dramatic centerpieces, and decorative garnishes. Brunch can also be a communal effort, a time when guests can help cook and serve.

Buffet or sit-down, indoors or out, brunch has become a weekend phenomenon from coast to coast, with each region developing its own brunch customs. In the New York metropolitan area, brunches are served close to noon. On the west coast and in the South, brunch is a midmorning meal. In some regions alcoholic drinks are taboo, while in others various drinks, such as champagne, or vodka mixed with fruit juices, are staples. Wherever you live, and whatever time of day you entertain, brunch, like any company meal, should be carefully prepared and presented to make it a special occasion. But it need not require hours of work in advance.

On the following pages, nine of America's most talented cooks present 27 complete menus featuring delicious brunches that can be made in an hour or less. They focus on light, casual meals that are nevertheless substantial enough to satisfy appetites from late morning until dinnertime. They use fresh produce, with no powdered sauces or other dubious shortcuts. The other ingredients (vinegars, spices, herbs, and so on) are all high quality, yet available for the most part in supermarkets or, occasionally, in a specialty shop. Each of the menus serves four people.

The photographs accompanying each meal show exactly how the dishes will look when you bring them to the table. The cooks and the test kitchen have planned the meals for

*A basket of eggs, a bowl of strawberries, and fresh asparagus, opposite, await preparation for brunch. Also on the countertop are other foods suitable for a midday meal (clockwise from top left): a pot of coffee with a container of cream, assorted fruit, a bottle of wine, crusty bread, and a platter of smoked salmon.*

## Coffee

Though wines and other alcoholic beverages are always optional at brunch, coffee is the one drink that almost always appears.

Three elements determine both the quality and taste of brewed coffee: the roasting time, the type of bean, and the brewing method. Roasting amplifies the inherent flavor and fragrance of green coffee beans. The length of roasting time determines the intensity of the beans' flavor. Light to medium roasts, which many Americans prefer, produce a mellow, delicate brew. Long-roasted beans produce the strong, robust coffees that Europeans and Middle Easterners drink. Italian espresso, produced from long-roasted beans, has a potent, almost-burnt taste.

Because characteristics vary, the type of coffee bean is another important determinant of taste. Colombian coffee beans produce a full-flavored yet delicate drink. By contrast, Sumatran Mandheling, Angolan, Mocha, Kenyan, or Brazilian beans are pungent and rich, and blend well with milder beans. Many serious coffee connoisseurs buy their favorite beans, or blend of beans, have them roasted to order, then grind the beans at home just before brewing each pot of coffee. Whether you buy whole roasted beans to grind at home or commercially ground coffee, remember that both become stale quickly. Store ground coffee in an airtight container in the refrigerator or freezer. It will retain flavor up to 4 months.

Whatever brewing method you use—percolator, drip, or vacuum—follow some basic rules. Metal pots can make coffee taste bitter, so use only glass or porcelain coffee makers. Use freshly ground coffee from quality beans, and start with cold, fresh water. Heat the water to just under the boiling point, about 205 degrees. If the water is at a full boil, it extracts a bitter taste from the coffee grounds. Select the correct grind for your brewing method: drip coffee requires a finer grind than percolated. Serve coffee as soon as it is brewed, and do not reheat it. Never boil coffee, and do not keep a filled coffee pot warming on a heating unit. The coffee will become bitter. To remove traces of oil, wash out coffee pots with a baking-soda-and-water solution after each use. Rinse thoroughly with water only.

For one cup of coffee, the standard ratio is 2 tablespoons of ground coffee to 1 cup water. You may prefer a different strength, so experiment with proportions.

The following recipes are for special coffees, which are particularly enjoyable at brunch.

*Café au lait:* Pour hot coffee and an equal amount of hot milk together into each cup or mug.

*Espresso:* Use espresso coffee that has been ground for use in American coffee makers. Use 10 tablespoons grounds to 2½ cups of water. Serve the coffee with a strip of lemon zest dropped into each cup.

*Mocha:* Pour equal amounts of hot coffee and hot chocolate into each cup. Sweeten to taste. Top with whipped cream, if desired, and shaved bittersweet chocolate.

*Mexican style:* Pour hot coffee into each cup and add a cinnamon stick. Top with whipped cream, if desired.

*Iced coffee:* Brew a fresh pot of strong coffee. Cool it, then chill it completely. Fill a tall glass or mug with ice cubes, then add the cold coffee. Top with a few tablespoons of heavy cream, if desired, and stir.

---

appearance as well as taste: the vegetables are brilliant and fresh, the visual combinations appetizing. The table settings feature bright colors, simple flower arrangements, and attractive, but not necessarily expensive, serving pieces. You can readily adapt your own tableware to these menus in convenient ways that will please you and your guests.

For each menu, the Editors, with advice from the cooks, suggest wines and other beverages—and various kinds of extra touches—to accompany the meals. And there are suggestions for the best uses for leftovers. On each menu page, too, you will find a range of other tips, from the best way to peel and segment an orange to the tricks for selecting the freshest produce. All the recipes have been tested meticulously to make sure that a relatively inexperienced cook can complete them within the time limit.

### BEFORE YOU START

*Great Meals in Minutes* is designed for efficiency and ease. The books will work best for you when you follow these suggestions:

1. Refresh your memory with the few simple cooking techniques on the following pages. They will quickly become second nature and will help you produce professional meals in minutes.

2. Read the menus *before* you shop. Each one opens with a list of all the required ingredients, listed in the order you would expect to shop for them in the average supermarket. Check for those few you need to buy; many items will already be on your pantry shelf.

3. Check the equipment list on pages 16–17. A good, sharp knife or knives and pots and pans of the right shape and material are essential for making great meals in minutes. This may be the time to look critically at what you own and plan to buy a few things. The right equipment can turn cooking from a necessity into a creative experience.

4. Get out everything you need before you start to cook: the lists at the beginning of each menu tell what is required. To save effort, keep your ingredients close at hand and always put them in the same place so you can reach for them instinctively.

5. Take meat and dairy products from the refrigerator early enough for them to come to room temperature; this will cut cooking time.

6. Follow the step-by-step game plan with each menu. That way, you can be sure of having the entire meal ready to serve at the right moment.

### TABLE SETTINGS

Because brunch is an uncomplicated and almost spontaneous meal, you can take time to indulge in some of the creative frills of entertaining: table arrangements, including dramatic centerpieces that are the table's focal point, and decorative garnishes to dress up your food.

When you are planning your gathering, decide whether you want a casual eat-when-you-want buffet or a more formal and structured sit-down meal. Take stock of your cupboard to determine if you have all the linens, plates, serving pieces, and vases you might want for creating a particular mood or for setting an attractive table. You do not need an extensive and costly inventory for brunch; for this kind of entertaining, you can carefully mix and match textures and colors of casual tableware. Perhaps this is the opportunity to buy some colorful informal ware: visit thrift shops, garage sales, or antique shops to fill in any gaps in your tableware.

Strive for a setting that you can achieve with some simple basics. Table linens, both place mats and tablecloths, set the stage. When selecting place mats, be imaginative: use straw, fabric, metal, or wooden mats in rectangles, rounds, or free-form shapes. Or, cover your table completely with a full-sized cloth. Consider a quilt, a floral-printed sheet, batik dress lengths, or ready-made table linens. You may decide to forego linens altogether, and serve brunch from the kitchen on individual trays.

### CENTERPIECES

Freshly cut flowers always make a dramatic centerpiece, but be willing to try something different—for example, one of the following suggestions. For a base, use a vase, tray, soup tureen, basket, bottle, or compote. As an attractive variant, use free-form pieces of driftwood to hold dried or silk flowers. To determine the right size centerpiece, set the table first to see how much space you have. In planning a sit-down meal, keep the composition either low, or tall and thin so your guests and you can easily converse. Whatever centerpiece you choose, key it to the menu, color scheme, and season.

### Silk, Ceramic, and Dried Flowers

Bright, delicate silk flowers are sumptuous and costly but look real and last indefinitely. Ceramic flowers are equally attractive; for extra appeal, choose some that are not exact copies of real flowers. Dried flowers, weeds, pods, and grasses are an inexpensive alternate to silk and fresh flowers but, because they are fragile, they may last only one season.

### Collectibles

If you collect seashells, driftwood, rocks, old bottles, miniature ceramics, or any other unusual or beguiling objects, display several as your centerpiece.

### Live Potted Plants

Singly or massed together, live plants in clay or ceramic pots look attractive any time of year. Set a large plant or several smaller plants on a decorative tray, mirrored square tiles, or coasters to prevent water and soil from leaking onto the table.

### Fruit and Vegetables

Straw baskets or decorative containers—pewter, silver,

---

### Making Crème Fraîche

Crème fraîche, which is an important part of the menus on pages 21, 37, and 100, is thickened cultured cream with a high butterfat content and a slightly tart, nutty taste unlike that of sweet or sour cream. It is a delicious topping for fruits and desserts and, when stirred into soups or sauces, both thickens and smooths them. Once a French specialty but now produced in the United States, crème fraîche is not only costly but difficult to find except at gourmet shops and certain supermarkets. However, there is no need to buy it, since you can make a reasonable approximation of crème fraîche at home, using the recipe below. It takes the mixture about 8 hours to thicken, so you must make it in advance.

#### Crème Fraîche

4 tablespoons buttermilk or 1 cup sour cream
2 cups heavy cream

**1.** In a heavy-gauge saucepan, combine the buttermilk or sour cream with the heavy cream. Heat over low heat just until the chill is removed and the mixture feels tepid to your finger (about 85 degrees).
**2.** Pour mixture into a glass jar and let stand at room temperature (ideally 75 degrees but no hotter than 85 degrees). It will thicken after about 6 to 8 hours.
**3.** When mixture is thick, stir, cover the jar, and refrigerate. The crème fraîche will last up to 10 days.

If you wish, you can now have a continuous supply of crème fraîche by adding the last of your "starter" (the crème fraîche you have on hand) to a new batch of heavy cream.

---

or ceramic—filled with fresh produce make colorful centerpieces. Fruit has a dual purpose: it is decorative, and can be eaten as part of, or after, the meal. An assortment of vegetables is particularly attractive when highlighted by vegetable greens such as carrot or beet tops, kale, parsley, or spinach. Greens last longer if crisped first: rinse and dry them, then wrap the leaves in moist paper towels, and refrigerate until ready to serve.

### GARNISHES

Carved fruits and vegetables, a form of table sculpture, make a meal memorable by enhancing both food and serving pieces. The only tools you need are a paring knife, a grooved knife (citrus zester), and a bowl of iced water for keeping cut produce fresh.

### Carved Fruits

*Zigzag cut:* for citrus halves. Cut a deep zigzag pattern around the circumference and through to the core and gently pull the halves apart.

*Scalloped slices:* for lemons, limes, or small oranges. With a grooved knife, peel off vertical strips of zest from one end of the orange to the other. Space the strips as you wish, but just keep them equidistant. Slice the fruit into rounds, and use the slices as they are. Or, for extra appeal,

9

Cooking at high temperatures can be dangerous, but not if you follow a few simple steps:

▶ Water added to hot fat will always cause spattering. If possible, pat foods dry with a cloth or paper towel before you add them to the hot oil in a skillet, Dutch oven, or wok.

▶ Lay the food in the pan gently, or the fat will certainly spatter.

▶ Be aware of your cooking environment. If you are boiling or steaming some foods while sautéing others, place the pots far enough apart so the water is unlikely to splash into the oil.

▶ Turn pot handles inward, toward the middle of the stove, so that you do not accidentally knock something over.

▶ Remember that alcohol—wine, brandy, or spirits—may occasionally catch fire when you add it to a very hot pan. If this happens, stand back for your own protection, and then quickly cover the pan with a lid. The fire will instantly subside, and the food will be just as good as ever.

▶ Keep pot holders and mitts close enough to be handy, but never hang them above the burners and do not lay them on the stove top.

remove one section of flesh so you can twist the slice into the shape of an "S."

*Strawberry fan:* for large, firm strawberries. Make three or four slices lengthwise, but not through the stem end, and then spread the slices out to form a fan. (See photograph on pages 22–23.)

*Half-moon loops:* for lemons, oranges, or limes. Slice fruit into ¼-inch rounds. Slice these rounds in half, then cut half the peel from the half round and loop it under itself. (See following diagrams.)

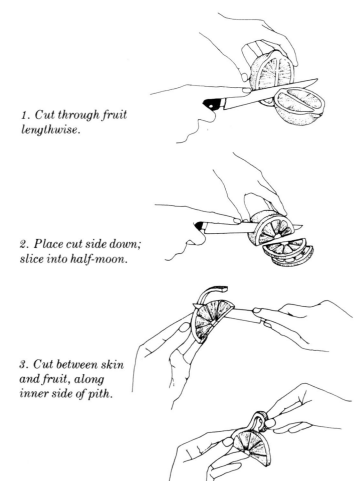

*1. Cut through fruit lengthwise.*

*2. Place cut side down; slice into half-moon.*

*3. Cut between skin and fruit, along inner side of pith.*

*4. Push rind back to form a loop.*

### Carved Vegetables

*Radish fans:* for large, firm radishes. Trim off the root, then cut thin slices from root end to stem end, taking care not to cut through the stem. Place the cut radish in warm, salted water for 10 minutes, or until the radish becomes pliable. Remove it from the water and spread out the slices to form a fan. (See following diagram.)

*Radish crosses:* Cut two thin slices from the center of the radish, leaving two round, even disks. Cut a notch into each slice and then slip the slices together at the notch. (See following diagram.)

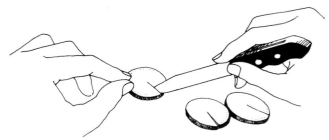

*1. Cut a notch in each radish slice.*

*2. Fit 2 slices together at the notches.*

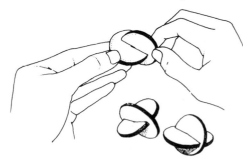

*Scallion brushes:* Cut off root ends and tops, leaving the scallion in 3-inch lengths. Place each one on a flat surface, and with the tip of a paring knife make three or four 1-inch cuts from the root end. Turn scallion 90 degrees and make a second set of cuts. Repeat at the leafy end, leaving about an inch of scallion uncut at its center. Drop in iced water and refrigerate until the cut ends curl out into brushlike fans.

*Tomato roses:* This looks complicated, but a tomato rose is one of the easiest garnishes to cut. Select a small, firm tomato or cherry tomato. Starting at the stem end, cut a strip ¼ to ½ inch wide, depending on the size of the tomato. Peel this strip of skin off the tomato in one continuous piece, rotating the tomato, as you cut, to follow its curve. Be careful to remove as little flesh from the tomato as possible. Beginning at the stem end, wrap the long peel around it in a spiral. This forms the "petals."

*Flowering tomatoes:* Cut firm cherry tomatoes into four quarters, without cutting entirely through the base. Peel back the skin from each quarter to the middle of the quarter. Leave some meat on the skin so that it furls out and looks as if it is flowering.

### COOKING TECHNIQUES

#### Sautéing
Sautéing is a form of quick frying, with no cover on the pan. In French, *sauter* means "to jump," which is what vegetables or small pieces of food do when you shake the sauté pan. The purpose is to lightly brown the food and seal in the juices, sometimes before further cooking. This technique has three critical elements: the right pan, the proper temperature, and dry food.

*The sauté pan:* A proper sauté pan is 10 to 12 inches in diameter and has 2- to 3-inch straight sides that allow you to turn food pieces and still keep the fat from spattering. It has a heavy bottom that slides easily over a burner.

The best material (and the most expensive) for a sauté pan is tin-lined copper because it is a superior heat conductor. Heavy-gauge aluminum works well but will discolor acidic food like tomatoes. Therefore, you should not use aluminum if the food is to be cooked for more than twenty minutes after the initial browning. Another option is to select a heavy-duty sauté pan made of strong, heat-conductive aluminum alloys. This type of professional cookware is smooth and stick-resistant.

The ultimate test of a good sauté pan is whether or not it heats evenly; hot spots will burn the food rather than brown it. A heavy sauté pan that does not heat evenly can be saved. Rub the pan with a generous amount of vegetable oil. Then place a half inch of salt in the pan and heat it slowly over low heat, about 10 to 15 minutes, until it is very hot. Empty out the salt, do not wash the pan, and rub it with vegetable oil again.

Select a sauté pan large enough to hold the pieces of food without crowding. The heat of the fat and the air spaces around and between the pieces facilitate browning. Crowding results in steaming—a technique that lets the juices out rather than sealing them in. If your sauté pan is not large enough to prevent crowding, separate the food into two batches, or use two pans at once.

Be sure you buy a sauté pan with a tight-fitting cover. Many recipes call for sautéing first, then lowering the heat and cooking the food, covered, for an additional 10 to 20 minutes. Make certain the handle is long and comfortable to hold.

Never immerse the hot pan in cold water; this will warp the metal. Allow the pan to cool slightly, then add water and let it sit until you are ready to wash it. Use a wooden spatula or tongs to keep food pieces moving in the pan as you shake it over the burner. If the food sticks, as it occasionally will, a metal spatula will loosen it best. Turn the pieces so that all surfaces come into contact with the hot fat and none of them sticks. Do not use a fork when sautéing meat; piercing the pieces will cause the juices to run out and will toughen the meat.

*The fat:* A combination of half butter and half vegetable oil or peanut oil is perfect for most sautéing; it heats to high temperatures without burning and allows you to have a rich butter flavor at the same time. Always use unsalted butter for cooking; it tastes better and does not add unwanted salt to your recipe.

Butter alone makes a wonderful-tasting sauté, but butter, whether salted or unsalted, burns at a high temperature. If you prefer an all-butter flavor, clarify the butter before you begin. This means removing the milky residue, which is the part that scorches. To clarify, heat the butter in a small saucepan over medium heat and, using a cooking

---

### Seasoning a Skillet

To produce perfect omelets and crêpes—such as for Margaret Fox's Filled Omelets (page 21) or for Bert Greene's Bloody Mary Crêpes (page 85)—you need well-seasoned, or nonstick, heavy-bottomed pans with sloping sides. You may choose aluminum, stainless steel, or cast-iron pans, but before using them, you must clean and season them well. The "seasoning" is a coat of oil permanently baked on the interior surface to prevent food from sticking. First rinse pans in warm water, scouring the inside surface with fine steel wool and soap. Rinse and dry the pan thoroughly. Then, pour a tablespoon of liquid cooking oil (corn, olive, peanut, or any vegetable oil) into a small bowl. Dip a pastry brush or paper towel into the oil, and coat the interior of the pan thoroughly. Wipe off any excess, then put the pan in a 300-degree oven for 30 to 60 minutes. Remove the pan from the oven and allow to cool. Before you cook your first omelet or crêpe, sprinkle a teaspoonful of salt into the pan, heat the pan, rub the inside well with a paper towel, and discard the salt. The pan is ready for use.

To clean, rub the pan with salt and a damp towel to remove any food residue. If you prefer, rinse the pan in warm, soapy water and dry it completely. Avoid scouring it or using harsh detergents. Rub the interior with a few drops of oil before you put the pan away.

If you scratch the surface with a metal cooking utensil, the pan will lose some of its seasoning, and you will need to repeat the seasoning process.

spoon, skim off the foam as it rises to the top and discard it. Keep skimming until no more foam appears. Pour off the remaining oil, making sure to leave the milky residue at the bottom of the pan. The oil is clarified butter: Use this for sautés.

Some sautéing recipes call for olive oil, which imparts a delicious and distinctive flavor of its own and is less sensitive than butter to high heat. Nevertheless, even the finest olive oil has some residue of fruit pulp, which will scorch at high heat. Watch the temperature carefully when you sauté in olive oil. Discard any scorched oil and start with fresh if necessary.

To sauté properly, heat the fat until it is hot but not smoking. When you see small bubbles on top of the fat, it is almost hot enough to smoke. In that case, lower the heat. When using butter and oil together, add the butter to the hot oil. After the foam from the melting butter subsides, you are ready to sauté. If the temperature is just right, the food will sizzle when you add it.

## Poaching

You poach fish or chicken, even fruit, exactly as you would an egg, in very hot liquid in a shallow pan on top of the stove. You can use water, or better still, chicken or fish stock, or a combination of stock and white wine, or even cream. Bring the liquid to the simmering point and add the food. Be prepared to lower the heat if the liquid begins to boil. Boiling toughens meat and dries it out. Poaching is an ideal summer cooking method, since it uses so little heat. See Ruth Spear's Oyster Pepper Pan Roast (page 34), and Maria Robbins's Ham Dumplings (page 41), for examples of poaching.

## Searing

Searing is somewhat like sautéing, but you need slightly hotter fat; when you sear, you brown the meat without shaking or stirring the pan. Heat the oil until it is very hot (at least 350 degrees), then brown the meat over high heat for a minute or two on each side. A metal spatula is essential, for the meat will tend to stick. Never pierce the meat; otherwise juices will be released and the meat will become dry and tough. Wait until it is very brown before you turn it.

## Deep-Fat Frying

People often say fry when they mean sauté. But frying calls for much more fat than does sautéing.

The best way to fry is to heat the fat slowly to between 360 and 375 degrees in a deep cast-iron skillet or other heavy, high-sided pan. Use a deep-fat thermometer or test the temperature by frying a small cube of bread—it should brown in less than a minute when the fat is hot enough. The temperature is important; underheating causes the food to absorb oil, and overheating scorches the food.

The fat should be vegetable or peanut oil; never use butter alone or a mostly butter mixture. Whatever fat you use, slide the food pieces gently into the pan, using a pair of tongs. Hot fat spatters dangerously if you drop food into it.

## Broiling and Grilling

These are two relatively fast ways to cook meat, poultry, and fish, giving the food a crisp exterior while leaving the inside juicy. For uniform cooking, flatten the pieces of food, especially chicken or game hens, to an even thickness. Whether broiling or grilling, brush meat with melted fat, a sauce, or a marinade before you cook. This adds flavor and keeps the food moist.

In broiling, the meat cooks directly under the heat source. To ensure that the meat is done before the surface burns, move the broiling rack five or six inches from the heat source.

In grilling, the food cooks directly over the heat source, which is frequently a bed of charcoal. Cooking pancakes on a well-seasoned cast-iron or stoneware griddle placed directly over a burner—another form of grilling—evolved from the griddle baking of the ancient Celts, who cooked breads on stone or iron slabs over an open fire. With the modern method, the griddle is heated until drops of cold water splashed on its surface jump. Shelley Handler cooks buckwheat cakes (page 95), and Margaret Fox cooks ricotta pancakes (page 24), using this method.

## Flambéing

Flambéing makes a dramatic point at any meal. It requires igniting a warm, but not close to boiling, liquor in the pan with already-cooked hot food. Be sure to remove the pan from the heat first; then avert your face and ignite the liquor with a lighted match. A quiet flame will burn for a few seconds. Henry Creel uses this method with his Bananas Flambée (page 79). Allow about an ounce of liquor per person with flambéing. The taste remains, but the alcohol burns off—and you have enjoyed a moment of showmanship.

## Roasting and Baking

Originally, *roasting* was the term for cooking meat on a revolving spit over an open fire, but now it means cooking

# Making Chicken Stock

Although canned chicken broth or stock is all right for emergencies, homemade chicken stock has a rich flavor that is hard to match. Moreover, the commercial broths—particularly the canned ones—are likely to be oversalted.

To make your own stock, save chicken parts as they accumulate and put them in a bag in the freezer; then have a rainy-day stock-making session, using one of the recipes here. The skin from a yellow onion will add color; the optional veal bone will add extra flavor and richness to the stock.

## Basic Chicken Stock

3 pounds bony chicken parts, such as wings, back, and neck
1 veal knuckle (optional)
3 quarts cold water
1 yellow unpeeled onion, stuck with 2 cloves
2 stalks celery with leaves, cut in two
12 crushed peppercorns
2 carrots, scraped and cut into 2-inch lengths
4 sprigs parsley
1 bay leaf
1 tablespoon fresh thyme, or 1 teaspoon dried
Salt (optional)

1. Wash chicken parts and veal knuckle (if you are using it) and drain. Place in large soup kettle or stockpot (any big pot) with the remaining ingredients—except salt. Cover pot and bring to a boil over medium heat.

2. Lower heat and simmer stock, partly covered, 2 to 3 hours. Skim foam and scum from top of stock several times. Add salt to taste after stock has cooked 1 hour.

3. Strain stock through fine sieve placed over large bowl. Discard chicken pieces, vegetables, and seasonings. Let stock cool uncovered (this will speed cooling process). When completely cool, refrigerate. Fat will rise and congeal conveniently at top. You may skim it off and discard it or leave it as protective covering for stock.

*Yield:* About 10 cups.

The flavor of chicken stock comes from the bones (as well as the seasonings and vegetables) rather than the meat. The longer you cook the bones, the better the stock. If you would like to poach a whole chicken and want to make a good, strong stock at the same time, this highly economical recipe will accomplish both aims at once.

## Strong Chicken Stock

10 cups homemade chicken stock (yield of recipe at left)
1 bay leaf
1 stalk celery
1 carrot, scraped
1 yellow onion, unpeeled
1 whole broiler or fryer (about 3 pounds)

1. Add stock, bay leaf, and vegetables to kettle large enough to hold them and chicken. Bring to a boil over medium heat.

2. Add chicken, breast up, and allow liquid to return to a simmer. Reduce heat and poach chicken with lid slightly ajar.

3. After 40 minutes, test for doneness. Insert long-handled spoon into chicken cavity and remove chicken to platter.

4. When chicken is cool enough to handle, but still warm, debone it, reserving meat for salads or sandwiches but returning skin and bones to cooking pot. Continue to simmer, uncovered, until stock has reduced by half. Proceed as in step 3 of basic stock recipe, left.

*Added Touch:* If you have time and want a particularly rich-looking stock, put the chicken bones in a shallow baking pan and brown them under the broiler for 10 minutes before you add them to the stock.

Stock freezes well and will keep for three months in the freezer. Use small containers for convenience and freeze in pre-measured amounts: a cup, or half a cup. Or pour the cooled stock into ice cube trays, then remove the frozen cubes and store in a plastic bag. You can drop these frozen cubes directly into your saucepan.

---

meat or poultry in an oven by a dry-heat process. Roasting is especially suitable for thick cuts of meat and whole poultry. You should baste meats several times with the drippings that collect in the pan.

*Baking* also means cooking food in the oven, but it is a much more versatile technique. You use it for preparing breads and raw vegetables like potatoes, as Maria Robbins does (page 47), for cooking a combination of ingredients as with Henry Creel's meat loaves (pages 76–77), or for salt baking, that is, burying meat, fish, or poultry in coarse salt.

## Braising
This method cooks food by moist heat but, unlike poaching or boiling, you generally brown the food well before combining it with the cooking liquid, which may be meat juice, meat stock, water, milk, or vegetable juices. Then you simmer the food and the liquid slowly over low heat in a tightly covered pot. Braising is a fine way to tenderize tough cuts of meat, and it also produces delicious vegetable dishes.

## Boiling
There are two basic boiling methods: With the first method, vegetables boil in a small amount of water in a covered pot. This minimizes nutrient loss and maximizes flavor retention, but it is necessary to watch the vegetables closely so that the water does not boil away.

The second, which professional cooks often use, calls for filling a large stockpot with water and bringing the water to a rolling boil. Boil the vegetables in an uncovered pot until they are tender but not soft. Drained immediately in a colander, they stop cooking. Serve them at once. Ideal for most green vegetables, quick boiling retains their color. Moreover, the intense flavor of vegetables such as cabbage disperses in a quantity of hot water. Both Maria Robbins (pages 43–44), and Bert Greene (page 88), prepare asparagus using this method.

# Pantry (for this volume)

A well-stocked, properly organized pantry is a time-saver for anyone who wants to prepare great meals in the shortest time possible. Location is the critical factor for staple storage. Whether your pantry consists of a small refrigerator and two or three shelves over the sink or a large freezer, refrigerator, and whole room just off the kitchen, you must protect staples from heat and light.

In maintaining or restocking your pantry, follow these rules:

1. Store staples by kind and date. Canned goods need a separate shelf, or a separate spot on the shelf. Put the oldest cans in front, so that you need not examine each one as you pull it out. Keep track of refrigerated and frozen staples by jotting the date on the package or writing it on a bit of masking tape.

2. Store flour, sugar, and other dry ingredients in canisters or jars with tight lids, where they will last for months. Glass and clear plastic allow you to see at a glance how much remains.

3. Keep a running grocery list near where you cook so that when a staple such as olive oil, sugar, or flour is half gone, you will be sure to stock up.

## ON THE SHELF:

### Anchovies
Anchovy fillets, both flat and rolled, come oil-packed, in tins. If you buy whole, salt-packed anchovies, they must be cleaned under running water, skinned, and boned. To bone, separate the fish with your fingers and slip out the backbone.

### Baking powder

### Baking soda

### Bouquet garni
This is an herb bouquet, composed of parsley, thyme, and bay leaf, used to flavor soups, stews, and the like. If you are using fresh herbs, tie them together with string; if dried, tie them in a square of washed cheesecloth. A *bouquet garni* is always removed from the dish before serving.

### Capers
Capers are usually packed in vinegar (and less frequently in salt). If you use those bottled in salt, you should rinse them under cold water before using them.

### Chicken (or beef) stock
Canned stock, or broth, is adequate for most recipes and convenient to have on hand, but you may prefer to make your own chicken stock (see page 13).

### Cornstarch

### Dried fruits
prunes
raisins

### Flours and meals
all-purpose
　Ground for any use from cakes to bread, it may be bleached or unbleached.
cornmeal
　May be yellow or white and of varying degrees of coarseness. The stone-ground variety is milled to retain the germ of the corn; it generally has a superior flavor.

### Herbs and spices
Fresh herbs are always best; the flavor is much better than in dried herbs. Many fresh herbs are now available at produce markets. If you like, you can grow basil, chervil, oregano, sage, and—depending on climate—several other herbs in a small garden outdoors or on a sunny windowsill. Fresh herbs should be used immediately. The following herbs and spices, however, are perfectly acceptable in dried or packaged form—but buy in small amounts and use as quickly as possible. In measuring herbs, remember that three parts of fresh herbs will equal one part dried. *Note:* Dried chives and parsley should not be on your shelf, since they have little or no flavor. But freeze-dried chives are acceptable.

allspice
basil, fresh and dried
caraway seeds
chervil
chives, fresh, freeze-dried or frozen
cinnamon, whole or ground
cloves, whole or ground
coriander
cumin
curry powder, preferably imported
dill, fresh and dried
fennel seeds
ginger (ground)
marjoram
mustard (dry)
nutmeg, whole or freshly ground
oregano
paprika
pepper
　*black, whole peppercorns*
　These are unripe peppercorns dried in their black skins. Grind with a pepper mill for each use.
　*Cayenne pepper*
　*ground red chili peppers*
　*red chili peppers, dried*
　*red pepper flakes*
　Also called crushed red pepper.
　*white, whole peppercorns*
　These are like the black variety but are picked unripe and dried without the skin. Use them in pale sauces when black pepper specks would spoil the appearance.
rosemary, fresh or dried
saffron

Made from the dried stamens of a species of crocus, this expensive seasoning adds both color and flavor.
sage
salt
　Use coarse—also known as Kosher—salt because of its superior flavor and coarse texture. It is pure salt with no additives. Kosher salt and sea salt taste saltier than table salt. When the recipe calls for Kosher or sea salt, you can substitute in the following proportions: three quarters teaspoon Kosher or sea salt equals one teaspoon table salt.

savory
sesame seeds
tarragon
thyme, leaf and ground

### Honey

### Hot pepper sauce

### Maple syrup

### Nuts, chopped or whole
almonds
pecans
walnuts

### Oils
corn, peanut, or vegetable
　Because these neutral oils add little or no taste to the food and have high smoking points, they are good for sautéing.
olive oil
　Sample French, Greek, Spanish, and Italian oils (Luccan oil, from the

14

Tuscan region, is sure to be in your supermarket) until you find the taste you like best. Each has its own flavor. Buy only virgin or first-pressing oil; the oil from the second pressing is full of fruit pulp that burns at high heat. Good olive oils may vary in color from green to golden yellow. The pale and less expensive oils are fine for cooking.

safflower oil
> The polyunsaturated type is especially favored by those on a low-cholesterol diet.

**Olives,** green and black

**Onions**
> Store all dry-skinned onions in a cool, dry place.

garlic
> The most pungent of the onion family. Garlic powder and garlic salt are no substitute for the real thing.

red onions
> Their sweet flavor makes them ideal for salads. They are rarely used for cooking because they are very mild.

scallions
> Also called green onions, they have a mild flavor. Use the white bulbs as well as the fresh green tops. Wrap in plastic and store in the refrigerator, or chop coarsely, wrap in plastic, and freeze.

shallots
> Use this sweet and delicate cross between onions and garlic chopped for best flavor. Buy the largest shallots you can find; they are easier to peel and chop.

Spanish onions
> Their sweet, delicate taste is good in onion soups or in sandwiches.

white onions
> Also called boilers or silver skins, these small round onions are suitable for cooking whole.

yellow onions
> These all-purpose cooking onions have a strong flavor—good for flavoring stock.

**Pasta and noodles,** dried or fresh
> Follow instructions on the package for cooking, add pasta to the pot slowly enough so that the boil is not interrupted, and avoid overcooking.

**Potatoes**

**Rice**

Arborio rice
> A plump, short-grain rice that turns creamy-firm when cooked, it is available in Italian groceries, specialty food stores, and some supermarkets.

long-grain white rice
> This is lighter and fluffier than short grain when cooked.

**Soy sauce**
> Buy the Japanese brands, which are very flavorful and less salty than Chinese and American soy sauces.

**Sugar**
> brown sugar
> confectioners' sugar
> granulated sugar

**Tomatoes**

Italian plum tomatoes
> For tomato sauces, canned plum tomatoes are an acceptable substitute for ripe tomatoes.

tomato paste
> This is also for sauces. With canned paste, spoon out unused portions in one-tablespoon amounts onto waxed paper and freeze, then lift the frozen paste off and store in a plastic container. Sometimes available in tubes, which can be refrigerated and kept for future use after a small amount is gone.

tomato sauce

**Vanilla extract**

**Vinegars**

apple cider vinegar (also called cider vinegar)
> Use when you want a mild, fruity flavor.

distilled white vinegar

red and white wine vinegars

> Use in cooking and in salad dressings.

sherry wine vinegar
> This is nutty and somewhat stronger flavored than most wine vinegars. Buy in specialty stores.

tarragon vinegar
> Simply a wine vinegar flavored with fresh tarragon, this is especially good in salads.

**Wines, liquors**
> Madeira
> sherry
> red wine, sweet and dry
> white wine, dry

**Worcestershire sauce**


## IN THE REFRIGERATOR:

**Bread crumbs**
> You need never buy these. For fresh bread crumbs, use fresh or day-old bread; for dry, use fresh to 4-day-old bread. To dry bread, toast in a 250-degree oven until golden. Process bread in a food processor or blender.

**Butter**
> Unsalted is best for cooking because it does not burn as quickly as salted, and it has a sweeter flavor. Can be kept frozen until needed.

**Cheese**
> cream cheese
> Parmesan cheese
>> Avoid the preground variety; it is very expensive and almost flavorless. Buy Parmesan by the half- or quarter-pound wedge and grate as needed: a quarter pound produces one cup of grated cheese. American Parmesans are acceptable and less costly than imported. Romano is another substitute—or try mixing the two.

> Swiss cheese
>> Emmenthaler or Gruyère

> ricotta cheese
>> This white, slightly sweet soft cheese, whose name means "recooked," is a by-product made from whey. It

is available fresh (made from whole milk) or dry. It resembles good-quality small curd cottage cheese, which can be substituted.

**Cream**
> half-and-half
> heavy cream
> light cream
> sour cream

**Crème fraîche,** commercial or homemade (see page 9)

**Eggs**
> Will keep up to 6 weeks. Before beating eggs, bring them to room temperature for fluffiest results.

**Ginger,** fresh
> Buy fresh in the produce section. Slice only what you need. The rest will stay fresh in the refrigerator for 6 weeks wrapped in plastic. Or place the whole ginger root in a small jar and cover it with dry sherry to preserve it. It will keep indefinitely. You need not peel ginger root.

**Lemons**
> In addition to its many uses in cooking, fresh lemon juice, added to cut fruits and vegetables, keeps them from turning brown. Added to the cooking water, lemon juice keeps rice from turning yellow as it cooks. Do not substitute bottled juice or lemon extract.

**Mustard**
> Select the pungent Dijon variety for cooking. The flavor survives heating. Dry mustard and regular hot dog mustard have their uses and their devotees, but the recipes in this book call for Dijon.

**Parsley**
> Put in a glass of water and cover loosely with a plastic bag. It will keep for a week in the refrigerator. Or you can wash it, dry it, and refrigerate it in a small plastic bag with a dry paper towel inside to absorb any moisture.

**Yogurt,** plain

# Equipment

Proper cooking equipment makes the work light and is a good cook's most prized possession. You can cook expertly without a store-bought steamer or even a food processor; but basic pans, knives, and a few other items are indispensable. Below are the things you need—and some attractive options—for preparing the menus in this volume.

## Pots and pans

Large kettle or stockpot

3 skillets (large, medium, small) with covers

Sauté pans, 10–12 inches in diameter, with covers and ovenproof handles

3 saucepans with covers (1-, 2-, and 4-quart capacities)
Choose enameled cast-iron, plain cast-iron, aluminum-clad stainless steel, and heavy aluminum (but you need at least one saucepan that is not aluminum). Best—but very expensive—is tin-lined copper.

Roasting pan with rack

2 shallow baking pans (8″ by 8″ by 2″ and 13″ by 9″ by 2″)

2 cookie sheets (11″ by 17″ and 15½″ by 12″)

Loaf pan (8½″ by 4¼″ by 3″)

2 soufflé dishes (1½-quart, 2-quart)

2- or 3-quart casserole with cover

9″ or 10″ pie plate

2 cake pans (9″ diameter)

## Knives

A carbon-steel knife takes a sharp edge but tends to rust. You must wash and dry it after each use; otherwise it can blacken food and counter tops. Good-quality stainless-steel knives, frequently honed, are less trouble and will serve just as well in the home kitchen. Never put a fine knife in the dishwasher. Rinse it, dry it, and put it away—but not loose in a drawer. Knives will stay sharp and last a long time if they have their own storage rack.

Small paring knife (sharp-pointed end)

10-inch chef's knife

Boning knife

Thin-bladed slicing knife

Sharpening steel

Bread knife (serrated edge)

## Other cooking tools

3 mixing bowls in graduated sizes

Flour sifter

Colander, with a round base (stainless steel, aluminum, or enamel)

Strainers (preferably 2, in fine and coarse mesh)

Sieve, coarse mesh

2 sets of measuring cups and spoons in graduated sizes ( one for dry ingredients, another for shortening and liquids)

Long-handled cooking spoon

Long-handled slotted spoon

Long-handled wooden spoons

Long-handled, 2-pronged fork

Wooden spatula (for stirring hot ingredients)

Metal spatula or turner (for lifting hot foods from pans)

Rubber or vinyl spatula (for folding in hot or cold ingredients, off the heat)

Grater (metal, with several sizes of holes)

Nutmeg grater

2 wire whisks

Pair of metal tongs

Wooden chopping board

Food mill, ricer, or potato masher

Vegetable steamer

Vegetable peeler

Mortar and pestle

Soup ladle

Nutcracker

Kitchen scissors

Kitchen timer

Aluminum foil

Cheesecloth

Paper towels

Plastic wrap

Wax paper

## Electric appliances

Blender or food processor
A blender will do most of the work required in this volume, but a food processor will do it more quickly and in larger volume. A food processor should be considered a necessity, not a luxury, for anyone who enjoys cooking.

Electric mixer

Toaster

## Optional

Griddle

Omelet pan

Double boiler

Gratin dish

9″ quiche dish, preferably porcelain

Muffin tin

Custard cups

Brioche molds

Copper bowl

Carving knife

Clam or oyster knife

Grapefruit knife (serrated edge)

Citrus juicer (inexpensive glass kind from the dime store will do)

Apple corer

Melon scoop

Pastry brush for basting (a small, new paintbrush that is not nylon serves well)

Wire skimmer

Pastry blender

Rolling pin

Flametamer or asbestos mat

Meat grinder

Salad spinner

Zester

Roll of masking tape or white paper tape for labeling and dating

STRAINER

SAUCEPANS

CASSEROLE

NUTMEG GRATER

SAUTÉ PAN

WHISK

PARING KNIFE

CHEF'S KNIFE

VEGETABLE STEAMER

SHARPENING STEEL

VEGETABLE PEELER

LONG-HANDLED WOODEN SPOON

SLOTTED METAL SPOON

METAL COLANDER

17

# Margaret Fox

MENU 1 (Left)
**Filled Omelets**
**Raspberries with Crème Fraîche**
**Buttermilk Coffeecake**

MENU 2
**Ricotta Pancakes**
**Scrambled Eggs with Herbs**
**Pork Sausages in White Wine**
**Melon Balls**

MENU 3
**Sautéed Ham and Cheese Sandwiches**
**Orange and Grapefruit Salad**

For Margaret Fox, cooking has been a lifelong preoccupation. Her mother taught her to experiment with food. Now a professional cook and restaurateur, Margaret Fox has developed an adventurous approach to developing new recipes.

Her free-and-easy cooking style was also influenced by the culinary daring of her fellow Californians, as well as the abundant and varied fresh produce of the state. "In the Mendocino area, where I live and work, local gardens supply the restaurant's produce, and my own garden supplies my herbs," she says. "Fresh foods must be simply yet creatively prepared. This allows their full tastes and textures to come through."

Breakfast is her favorite meal, and lunch a close second; brunch, which combines the best of both, can be as plain or fancy as the cook chooses. The omelet party of Menu 1 exemplifies how flexible brunch can be. Guests can congregate in the kitchen while the cook prepares the omelets and select the fillings they prefer: either the smoked salmon with cream cheese and new potatoes or the toasted walnuts with cheese and new potatoes. As a garnish for the omelets, the cook suggests using nasturtiums fresh from the garden.

In Menu 2, with ricotta cheese pancakes and herbed scrambled eggs, and in Menu 3, with the sautéed ham and cheese sandwiches, Margaret Fox shows how inventiveness transforms familiar foods.

*For a participatory brunch, set up a table in the kitchen and cook each omelet to order. Each guest can choose his or her own omelet filling: either cream cheese, sour cream, and smoked salmon; or sour cream, toasted walnuts, and Gruyère. Each is topped with sautéed new potatoes. Offer a basket of raspberries with a pitcher of crème fraîche and pass the buttermilk coffee cake in a napkin-lined bread basket.*

19

# Filled Omelets
# Raspberries with Crème Fraîche
# Buttermilk Coffeecake

Serve this brunch informally, in the kitchen, so that guests can begin to eat as soon as the omelets are ready. Cooking a perfect omelet takes just 30 to 60 seconds. The only trick is to keep the eggs from sticking to the pan. Because the eggs must be able to move around freely, a well-seasoned heavy-gauge skillet or nonstick pan is essential. Ideally, you should reserve it exclusively for omelets, crêpes, and scrambled eggs. Without a reliable pan, you cannot keep the omelet intact as you remove it from the pan.

Have each guest choose his or her omelet filling in advance. Then, when the edge of the omelet is firm but the center is still creamy, add the chosen filling.

If you have leftover fillings, cover and refrigerate them for use the next day. Spread cream cheese on freshly toasted English muffins or bagels; top with salmon strips. The walnut and cheese mixture makes a delicious dip.

Unless you can find commercial crème fraîche, the dessert of ripe raspberries and crème fraîche will require some ahead-of-time preparation. Make the crème fraîche the night before according to the recipe on page 9. If fresh raspberries are out of season, serve strawberries or poached apples or pears along with the crème fraîche.

## WHAT TO DRINK

Try a good Italian Soave or a French Sancerre here: either should be served chilled.

## SHOPPING LIST AND STAPLES

8 ounces smoked salmon
4 strips bacon
8 small red potatoes
Small bunch scallions
1 pint raspberries
1 stick unsalted butter
13 eggs
1 cup buttermilk
2 cups crème fraîche, preferably homemade (see page 9), or commercial
½ pint sour cream
½ pound cream cheese, preferably unpasteurized
¼ pound Gruyère cheese
1 cup corn oil
Hot pepper sauce
2¼ cups all-purpose flour

1 teaspoon baking soda
1 teaspoon baking powder
¾ cup granulated sugar
1 cup brown sugar
¾ cup shelled walnuts
1 cup sliced almonds
2 teaspoons cinnamon
¼ teaspoon ground ginger
Salt

## UTENSILS

Large heavy-gauge skillet
9-inch nonstick or well-seasoned omelet pan
Large saucepan
Small saucepan
Large sauté pan
13-by-9-by-2-inch baking pan
15½-by-12-inch cookie sheet
2 large bowls
Medium-size bowl
2 small bowls
Colander
Measuring cups and spoons
Chef's knife
Metal spatula
Rubber spatula
Wooden spoon
Cheese grater
Wire whisk (optional)
Wire cooling rack
Electric mixer

## START-TO-FINISH STEPS

*The morning before:* Make crème fraîche (see page 9), if desired. Refrigerate overnight.

**1.** Follow coffeecake recipe steps 1 through 4.
**2.** While coffeecake is baking, follow potato filling recipe step 1 and walnut filling recipe steps 1 and 2.
**3.** Follow potato filling recipe steps 2 and 3.
**4.** Follow salmon filling recipe steps 1 and 2.
**5.** Follow walnut filling recipe step 3 and potato filling recipe step 4.
**6.** Follow coffeecake recipe step 5 and potato filling recipe step 5.
**7.** Follow omelets recipe steps 1 through 3, walnut filling

recipe step 4, and salmon filling recipe step 3.
8. Follow coffeecake recipe step 6.
9. For dessert, follow raspberries recipe steps 1 and 2.

---

## RECIPES

### Filled Omelets

12 eggs
¼ cup cold water
6 drops hot pepper sauce
Salt
4 tablespoons unsalted butter
Omelet fillings (see following recipes)

1. Break eggs into large bowl and add water, hot pepper sauce, and salt to taste. Using fork or whisk, beat until well blended. Do not overbeat.
2. In nonstick or well-seasoned omelet pan, melt 1 tablespoon butter over medium-high heat. When foam subsides, pour in one quarter of egg mixture. Keeping pan close to burner, swirl mixture in circular motion 30 to 60 seconds, or until cooked, at which point bottom of omelet should be set and top should still be somewhat creamy. For a drier omelet, cook about 30 seconds longer.
3. Remove pan from heat and quickly spoon choice of filling—either smoked salmon and cheese or toasted walnuts and cheese—down one side of omelet; top either filling with sautéed potatoes. Using metal spatula, fold omelet in half; turn onto warm plate. Serve immediately. Repeat process for remaining omelets.

### Smoked Salmon Filling

½ pound cream cheese, preferably unpasteurized
¼ cup sour cream
8 drops hot pepper sauce
8 ounces smoked salmon

1. In medium-size bowl, combine cream cheese, sour cream, and hot pepper sauce. Using electric mixer, beat until thoroughly blended.
2. Cut salmon into ¼-inch strips.
3. Fill omelet by spooning one quarter of cheese mixture on one half. Top with strips of smoked salmon and one quarter of potato mixture.

### Toasted Walnuts and Cheese Filling

¾ cup shelled walnuts
4 strips bacon
¼ pound Gruyère cheese
¼ cup sour cream

1. Place walnuts on cookie sheet and toast in oven 5 to 10 minutes, shaking occasionally, until light brown.
2. While walnuts are toasting, cook bacon in skillet until crisp and drain on paper towels. With cheese grater or food processor, grate cheese. Set aside until ready to assemble omelet.
3. Remove walnuts from oven, cool slightly, and chop.

Crumble bacon. In small bowl, toss chopped walnuts, cheese, and bacon.
4. To fill omelet, spread 1 tablespoon sour cream on one half, then top with one quarter of walnut mixture and sautéed potatoes.

### Sautéed Potato Filling

8 small red potatoes
Small bunch scallions
4 tablespoons butter
4 tablespoons corn oil

1. In large saucepan, bring 2 quarts water to a boil.
2. Cook potatoes until tender, about 15 minutes. Drain in colander.
3. While potatoes are cooking, wash scallions and trim off root ends. Finely chop enough scallions to measure ½ cup.
4. When potatoes are cool enough to handle, cut into ½-inch cubes.
5. In large sauté pan, heat butter and oil over medium heat. Add scallions and potatoes, and cook, tossing frequently, until potatoes are crisp and lightly browned.

### Raspberries with Crème Fraîche

2 cups fresh raspberries
2 cups crème fraîche, preferably homemade

1. In colander, rinse raspberries briefly in cool water and drain. Gently pat dry with paper towels.
2. Turn into bowl and serve with pitcher of crème fraîche.

### Buttermilk Coffeecake

2¼ cups all-purpose flour
½ teaspoon salt
2 teaspoons cinnamon
¼ teaspoon ground ginger
1 cup brown sugar, firmly packed
¾ cup granulated sugar
¾ cup corn oil
1 cup sliced almonds
1 teaspoon baking soda
1 teaspoon baking powder
1 egg, beaten
1 cup buttermilk

1. Preheat oven to 350 degrees.
2. In large bowl, combine flour, salt, 1 teaspoon cinnamon, ginger, brown sugar, granulated sugar, and corn oil. Using fork, stir to combine.
3. To make topping, transfer ¾ cup of flour mixture to small bowl. Stir in almonds and remaining teaspoon of cinnamon, and set aside.
4. To make batter, add baking soda, baking powder, egg, and buttermilk to the remaining flour mixture. Mix batter until smooth and pour into buttered baking pan. Sprinkle evenly with reserved topping. Bake 35 to 40 minutes.
5. Cool slightly in pan on wire rack.
6. Cut into squares and serve warm.

# Ricotta Pancakes / Scrambled Eggs with Herbs
## Pork Sausages in White Wine
## Melon Balls

This substantial brunch features three main dishes: scrambled eggs with herbs, pork sausages, and ricotta pancakes, the last a favorite of the Fox family for years. Ricotta is a moist, bland, white cheese that resembles cottage cheese in appearance but tastes sweeter and richer. Ricotta is widely available at most supermarkets and Italian groceries. When combined with cottage cheese in a pancake batter, it produces rich, creamy pancakes. Prepare the batter just before serving time so that the stiffly beaten egg whites, gently folded into the batter,

*Melon balls, scrambled eggs, wine-simmered sausages, and ricotta pancakes look appealing on bright pottery. If you wish, garnish the main-dish plate with an orange slice and a strawberry.*

have no chance to deflate before being cooked.

To make creamy scrambled eggs, gently whisk the eggs until the whites and yolks are combined but not frothy. Heat the butter until it foams and add the herbs to the hot butter before you pour in the eggs. The heat releases the flavor of the herbs. Margaret Fox recommends using tarragon, thyme, or chives. Cook the eggs gently as the soft curds form, and take the eggs off the heat while they are still soft, since they will continue to cook in their own heat for about a minute.

The plate with the scrambled eggs and sausages can be dressed up easily with a quick, simple-to-do garnish, as shown in the photograph. Cut orange slices in half; then, with a small sharp knife, cut V-shaped notches along the

rim of each half, through both rind and pith. See page 10 for "strawberry fan" instructions.

## WHAT TO DRINK

Buy either a white or a red wine to accompany this brunch: a California Pinot Blanc for the white or an Italian Valpolicella for the red.

## SHOPPING LIST AND STAPLES

8 fresh pork sausage links, preferably country-style
Small ripe honeydew melon
Small ripe cantaloupe
Small bunch combined fresh basil, tarragon, chives, and
    parsley, or 1 teaspoon dried basil and tarragon
1 stick plus 4 tablespoons unsalted butter
1 dozen eggs
1 cup milk
8-ounce container ricotta cheese
8-ounce container small-curd cottage cheese
Pure maple syrup
Hot pepper sauce
⅔ cup all-purpose flour
1½ teaspoons baking powder

Salt
1 cup dry white wine

## UTENSILS

Griddle or large heavy-gauge skillet
10-inch skillet, preferably nonstick
8-inch skillet or sauté pan with ovenproof handle
4 large bowls
Ovenproof platter
Measuring cups and spoons
Chef's knife
Paring knife
Metal spatula
Wooden spatula with straight edge
Rubber spatula
Wire whisk
4-ounce ladle or cup
Melon ball cutter
Flour sifter
Electric mixer

## START-TO-FINISH STEPS

1. Follow pancakes recipe steps 1 through 3.

23

2. Follow sausages recipe steps 1 and 2.

3. While sausages are cooking, chop fresh herbs, if using, for eggs recipe and follow melon recipe steps 1 and 2.

4. Follow sausages recipe steps 3 and 4.

5. While sausages continue to cook, follow pancakes recipe steps 4 and 5 and eggs recipe steps 1 and 2.

6. Follow sausages recipe step 5 and eggs recipe step 3.

7. Follow pancakes recipe step 6 and serve with the sausages and eggs.

8. For dessert, follow melon balls recipe step 3.

---

RECIPES

## Ricotta Pancakes

⅔ cup unsifted all-purpose flour
1½ teaspoons baking powder
¼ teaspoon salt
4 eggs
1 cup ricotta cheese
⅓ cup small-curd cottage cheese
¾ cup plus 2 tablespoons milk
1 stick butter
Maple syrup

1. Preheat oven to 200 degrees. Onto a sheet of wax paper, sift together flour, baking powder, and salt.

2. Separate eggs into 2 large bowls. Add ricotta, cottage cheese, and milk to yolks and beat with electric mixer until blended. Gradually add flour mixture and beat just until well combined. Do not overbeat.

3. Wash and dry beaters. Beat egg whites until stiff but not dry. With rubber spatula, gently fold them into pancake batter just until combined. Cover and refrigerate until ready to make pancakes.

4. When ready to proceed, heat griddle or large heavy-gauge skillet over medium-high heat until a drop of water evaporates on contact.

5. Lightly grease griddle or skillet with shortening and pour out ¼ cup batter for each pancake. When bubbles form and break on surface, turn pancakes with metal spatula. Continue to cook about 2 minutes, or until undersides are golden brown. Using metal spatula, transfer to ovenproof platter and keep warm in oven. Cook remaining pancakes in the same manner, adding more shortening as necessary.

6. Remove pancakes from oven and serve hot with butter and maple syrup.

## Scrambled Eggs with Herbs

8 eggs
6 to 8 drops hot pepper sauce
3 tablespoons cold water
1 tablespoon combined chopped fresh basil, tarragon, chives, and parsley, or 1 teaspoon dried basil and tarragon
2 tablespoons unsalted butter

1. In large bowl, whisk together eggs, hot pepper sauce, cold water, and herbs just until combined. Do not overbeat. Place individual plates in oven to warm.

2. In 10-inch skillet, melt butter over medium-high heat.

3. When foam has subsided, reduce heat to medium, quickly pour in eggs, and, using wooden spatula, scramble eggs briskly, stirring from bottom of pan. When eggs have formed a solid mass but are still creamy, remove skillet from heat. Divide eggs among the warmed plates.

## Pork Sausages in White Wine

1 cup dry white wine
8 fresh pork sausage links, preferably country-style
2 tablespoons butter

1. In 8-inch skillet or sauté pan, bring wine to a boil over high heat. With fork, prick sausages in several places to prevent skins from bursting.

2. Lower heat to medium-low and add sausages. Cover and simmer gently 10 minutes.

3. Remove cover and turn heat up. Rapidly reduce wine until almost evaporated.

4. Lower heat and add butter to pan. Sauté sausages gently until they are richly browned, turning frequently, about 10 minutes.

5. Remove sausages from heat and keep warm in 200-degree oven until ready to serve.

## Melon Balls

1 honeydew melon
1 cantaloupe

1. With chef's knife, cut both melons in half; scoop out seeds.

2. Using melon ball cutter, scoop out rounds of fruit. Place in large bowl, mix together, and refrigerate until ready to serve.

3. To serve, divide fruit among 4 dessert bowls.

# Sautéed Ham and Cheese Sandwiches
# Orange and Grapefruit Salad

*A French-toast-style ham and cheese sandwich accompanies the orange, grapefruit, and red onion salad, garnished with carrot and scallion. Dark-colored plates provide a contrasting background for the food.*

25

A sautéed ham and cheese sandwich, an adaptation of the French *Croque Monsieur*, is the entrée for this brunch. Prepare the bread slices as for French toast: soak them in an egg-milk mixture, then brown them on a hot, buttered griddle or in a large skillet. Use firm-textured white bread that will not crumble during soaking. The cheese filling consists of grated Gruyère and crème fraîche. Use leftover crème fraîche from Margaret Fox's Menu 1, or make it following the recipe on page 9.

Tart orange and grapefruit sections, served in a mild vinaigrette, complement the rich egg taste of the sandwich. To peel both citrus fruits simply, place the whole fruit, stem end up, on a cutting board. With a sharp paring knife, cut off peel and white pith in one continuous strip, turning the fruit to follow its curve. Afterward, holding the fruit in one hand, separate each segment with the knife blade (see illustration on page 47).

For the vinaigrette, use a good-quality olive oil. The extra-virgin grade, though costly, has the fullest flavor. Japanese rice wine vinegar, a mild yet crisp vinegar, is a substitute for sherry wine vinegar, which may be difficult to find.

## WHAT TO DRINK

A light-bodied wine, such as a dry rosé from California or a Beaujolais, served lightly chilled, is in order here.

## SHOPPING LIST AND STAPLES

4 slices cooked ham
Small head Romaine lettuce
Small red onion
1 clove garlic
1 grapefruit
1 navel orange
4½ tablespoons unsalted butter
1 cup milk
4 eggs
½ pound Gruyère cheese
½ cup crème fraîche, preferably homemade (see page 9), or sour cream
½ cup light olive oil
2 tablespoons plus 1 teaspoon Dijon mustard
8 slices firm white bread, preferably day-old
Freshly ground nutmeg
Freshly ground white pepper

Salt
Freshly ground black pepper
2 tablespoons sherry wine vinegar or Japanese rice wine vinegar

## UTENSILS

Food processor or grater
Large griddle or large skillet plus additional large skillet (optional)
Large, shallow baking dish
2 small bowls
2 large bowls
2 large plates
Measuring cups and spoons
Chef's knife
Paring knife
Spatula
Wooden spoon
Wire whisk
Salad spinner (optional)

## START-TO-FINISH STEPS

1. Follow salad recipe steps 1 through 5.
2. Follow sandwich recipe steps 1 through 6.
3. After turning sandwiches, or after turning last two if cooking in two shifts, follow salad recipe step 6.
4. Serve salad with sandwiches.

## RECIPES

### Sautéed Ham and Cheese Sandwiches

½ pound Gruyère cheese
½ cup crème fraîche or sour cream
2 tablespoons Dijon mustard
4½ tablespoons unsalted butter
4 slices cooked ham
1 cup milk
4 eggs
Dash of salt
Pinch of freshly ground nutmeg
Freshly ground white pepper
8 slices firm white bread, preferably day-old

1. Preheat oven to 200 degrees. In food processor fitted with shredding disk or with cheese grater, grate Gruyère.

2. In small bowl, combine grated cheese, crème fraîche, and mustard.

3. In large skillet, melt ½ tablespoon of the butter. Add ham slices and brown quickly over medium heat, about 3 to 5 minutes. Transfer to paper-towel-lined plate and set aside.

4. In large bowl, whisk together milk, eggs, salt, nutmeg, and white pepper to taste until blended. Turn into large, shallow baking dish. Briefly soak the bread in the milk-and-eggs mixture just until saturated. Do not let it become soggy. Carefully remove slices and set aside on large plate.

5. Unless you have a griddle or 2 skillets large enough to cook 4 sandwiches at once, you will have to cook the sandwiches in shifts, keeping two warm in the oven as you complete the other two. On griddle or in the skillet used for the ham, heat 2 tablespoons of the butter over medium heat. Arrange 4 slices of the soaked bread in a single layer. Cook until golden brown on bottom, about 3 to 4 minutes, then turn. Divide half of cheese mixture between 2 slices. Reduce heat to low, cover pan, and allow cheese to melt, about 2 to 3 minutes.

6. Remove cover and place 1 slice of ham on each cheese-topped bread slice. Top with the bread slices remaining in pan and lightly press with spatula. Transfer sandwiches to individual plates. Keep warm in oven while preparing remaining sandwiches in same manner. Serve hot.

## Orange and Grapefruit Salad

Small head Romaine lettuce
1 clove garlic
2 tablespoons sherry wine vinegar, or Japanese rice wine vinegar
1 teaspoon Dijon mustard
½ cup light olive oil
Salt
Freshly ground pepper
Small red onion
1 grapefruit
1 navel orange

1. Wash lettuce thoroughly and dry in salad spinner or pat dry with paper towels. Refrigerate.

2. Peel and mince garlic. In small bowl, prepare vinaigrette by whisking together vinegar, mustard, garlic, olive oil, and salt and pepper to taste.

3. Peel onion and slice into thin rings. Add onion rings to vinaigrette and allow to marinate.

4. With paring knife, trim peel and white pith from grapefruit. Then, over large bowl, holding grapefruit in one hand and knife in other, free segments by cutting toward center on each side of the membranes, letting segments fall into bowl.

5. Peel and section orange in same manner. Cover bowl and refrigerate fruit until ready to serve.

6. When ready to serve, remove onion rings from vinaigrette and reserve. Arrange lettuce leaves on each plate and top with grapefruit and orange segments. Drizzle vinaigrette over fruit and garnish with the marinated onion rings.

---

### ADDED TOUCH

Because this meal is light, the editors suggest a moist cake as a good follow-up. The combination of cocoa and grated carrots creates an unusual and satisfying variation on carrot cake.

## Chocolate Carrot Cake

2½ cups all-purpose flour
½ cup unsweetened cocoa
2½ teaspoons baking powder
1½ teaspoons baking soda
1½ teaspoons salt
1½ teaspoons cinnamon
1 stick plus 4 tablespoons unsalted butter, at room temperature
2 cups sugar
3 eggs
1 teaspoon vanilla
½ cup milk
2 cups grated carrots
1 cup coarsely chopped walnuts (optional)

1. Preheat oven to 350 degrees.
2. Lightly grease and flour two 9-by-5-inch loaf pans.
3. In medium-size mixing bowl, combine flour, cocoa, baking powder, baking soda, salt, and cinnamon.
4. In large bowl, cream butter. Gradually beat in sugar. Add eggs, one at a time, beating well after each addition. Add vanilla and milk.
5. Alternately mix in dry ingredients and grated carrots. Mix in chopped walnuts, if using.
6. Divide batter between pans. Bake 45-55 minutes, or until a toothpick tests clean.

# Ruth Spear

Ruth Spear advises novices to concentrate on learning how to prepare the basics, then to evolve their own cooking styles. Each menu should be dictated by the seasonal availability of ingredients. Then the cook should select the main dish, building the rest of the menu around it, balancing tastes, textures, and colors.

Ruth Spear follows her own advice. When she invites company for Sunday brunch, which she serves at lunchtime, her meals are light and effortless, and geared to a season, as in Menu 3, which is suitable for fall or spring. Its main course of spaghetti stirred with julienned ham and tongue is topped by sautéed scallops and accompanied by a tossed green salad and by a fruit dessert of raspberries and kiwi. Menu 1, a meatless meal, features autumnal red bell peppers in a quiche, crisp spinach salad, and a tricolored dessert of strawberries, oranges, and pineapple—a visually balanced meal.

In Menu 2 the oyster pepper pan roast, despite its name, is a recipe in which the oysters cook gently but rapidly in butter. The accompanying beet and endive salad should be ready to serve before you start cooking the oysters.

*A red-pepper quiche is the main dish in this festive brunch. The spinach salad, inspired by a popular Japanese dish, has a soy-sauce-based dressing and contains toasted sesame seeds. Mandarin orange segments are an optional garnish. Arrange fruit salad components—strawberries, sectioned oranges, and pineapple chunks—using the shell of half the pineapple as a base. If you wish, garnish the fruit with mint leaves.*

# Red-Pepper Quiche
# Spinach Salad with Sesame Seeds
# Fresh Fruits in Liqueur

Red bell peppers are the principal ingredient for the rich, custardy quiche. Choose peppers that are firm, brightly colored and have no soft or wilted spots. Store them in a plastic bag in your refrigerator; they keep up to one week. The quiche also contains grated Swiss (Emmenthaler) or Gruyère, both whole-milk cheeses with a nutty flavor. When you make the quiche dough, allow 30 minutes for it to chill. In fact, if you wish, the quiche dough may be rolled out and fitted into the pan and all the filling ingredients assembled ahead of time, on the morning of your brunch.

The spinach salad features two ingredients often used in Asian cookery: soy sauce and sesame seeds. Soy sauce, made from fermented soybeans, adds both color and flavor to this salad, and sesame seeds, available in well-stocked supermarkets or in health-food stores, add a delightful nutty crunch.

To select a ripe pineapple for the third-course fruit cup, buy a heavy one with a deep golden rind. Its crown leaves should be dark green, and its center leaves should pull out easily. The chilled fruits are sprinkled with Cointreau, an orange-flavored liqueur. You may also use other orange liqueurs, such as Curaçao, Grand Marnier, or Triple Sec.

## WHAT TO DRINK

A crisp, well-chilled white wine would match the slight touch of sweetness in this menu; try a German Riesling or a bone-dry Verdicchio.

## SHOPPING LIST AND STAPLES

1 pound spinach
2 large, sweet red bell peppers
1 onion
Small bunch combined tarragon and parsley or parsley and dill
Small bunch mint (optional)
1 small pineapple
1 pint strawberries
1 orange, preferably seedless
4 eggs
½ cup milk
1 stick plus 1 tablespoon unsalted butter
½ pint heavy cream
¼ pound imported Swiss (Emmenthaler) or Gruyère cheese

2 tablespoons peanut oil
2 tablespoons soy sauce
1 cup unbleached flour
4 tablespoons sugar, preferably superfine, plus 2 teaspoons granulated
2 ounces sesame seeds
Cayenne pepper
Salt
¾ cup dry white wine
¼ cup Cointreau

## UTENSILS

Food processor (optional)
Small skillet
Small saucepan
Medium-size sauté pan
15½-by-12-inch cookie sheet
9- or 9½-inch porcelain quiche pan or metal tart tin
3 large bowls (or 2 if using processor)
2 small bowls
Measuring cups and spoons
Chef's knife
Paring knife
Slotted metal spoon
2 wooden spoons
Rubber spatula
Wire whisk
Cheese grater (if not using processor)
Rolling pin (optional)
Pastry cutter (if not using processor)
Salad spinner (optional)

## START-TO-FINISH STEPS

*One hour ahead:* follow pastry shell recipe steps 1 and 2.

1. Using food processor or cheese grater, grate cheese, peel and slice onion, chop herbs, and follow quiche recipe steps 1 through 3.
2. Follow pastry shell recipe step 3.
3. Follow quiche recipe steps 4 through 6.
4. While quiche is baking, follow fruits recipe steps 1 through 3 and spinach salad recipe steps 1 through 3.
5. Follow fruits recipe step 4.
6. Follow spinach salad recipe step 4, remove quiche from oven, and serve with salad.
7. For dessert, follow fruits recipe step 5.

## Red-Pepper Quiche

2 large, sweet red bell peppers
3 tablespoons unsalted butter
¾ cup thinly sliced onion
1⅓ cups grated Swiss (Emmenthaler) or Gruyère cheese
Pastry shell (see following recipe)
4 eggs
1 cup heavy cream
½ cup milk
½ cup combined chopped tarragon and parsley or parsley and dill
1 teaspoon salt
Cayenne pepper

1. Preheat oven to 350 degrees. Place cookie sheet in oven on middle rack.
2. Core and seed peppers. Remove membranes and cut lengthwise into ½-inch strips.
3. In sauté pan, heat 1 tablespoon of the butter over medium heat. Add onion and sauté until soft and faintly golden. Turn into small bowl. In same pan, melt remaining 2 tablespoons of butter. Add red peppers and sauté until they begin to brown, about 5 minutes. Remove pan from heat.
4. Sprinkle cheese evenly over bottom of pastry shell. Follow with a layer of onions and, using slotted spoon to transfer them, top with peppers. Reserve pan juices.
5. In large bowl, whisk together reserved pan juices, eggs, cream, milk, herbs, salt, and Cayenne to taste. Pour half of mixture into pastry shell. Place quiche on cookie sheet in oven and carefully pour in remainder of mixture.
6. Bake 45 minutes, or until golden and puffed. The quiche will sink somewhat as it cools.

## Pastry Shell

1 cup unbleached flour
1 teaspoon salt
6 tablespoons butter, chilled and cut into small pieces
3 to 4 tablespoons ice water

1. In food processor fitted with metal blade or in large mixing bowl, combine flour and salt. If using processor, process briefly. Add butter and pulse on and off until mixture resembles coarse meal. Add water in small amounts and pulse on and off just until pastry forms a ball. If not using processor, stir together flour and salt. With pastry cutter or 2 knives, blend butter until texture is crumbly. Slowly add water, blending quickly, just until pastry forms a ball.
2. Wrap dough in wax paper or plastic wrap. Chill at least 30 minutes or as long as overnight, if desired.
3. If dough has chilled for a long time, it may need to be softened before being pressed or rolled out. While it is still wrapped in wax paper, smack it a few times with your rolling pin to make it more pliable. To line the quiche pan quickly, simply press dough into it. Or, if you wish, roll dough out on a lightly floured board and fit into quiche pan.

## Spinach Salad with Sesame Seeds

2 tablespoons soy sauce
2 teaspoons granulated sugar
2 tablespoons peanut oil
¼ cup sesame seeds
1 pound spinach

1. In small saucepan, combine soy sauce, sugar, and oil. Cook over low heat, stirring, just until sugar dissolves. Remove pan from heat and cool.
2. In small skillet, toast sesame seeds over medium heat, shaking pan, until they brown slightly and start to pop. Remove pan from heat. If you wish to crush sesame seeds, place them between 2 pieces of wax paper and push a rolling pin over them. Stir seeds into cooled sauce.
3. In large bowl, wash spinach thoroughly in several changes of cool water to remove any grit. Dry in salad spinner or pat dry with paper towels. Discard stems and any wilted leaves. Wrap in paper towels and refrigerate until ready to assemble salad.
4. Transfer spinach to salad bowl. Stir sauce to recombine and pour over spinach. Toss until well coated. Serve with quiche.

## Fresh Fruits in Liqueur

1 orange, preferably seedless
1 pint strawberries
1 small pineapple
3 to 4 tablespoons sugar, preferably superfine
¾ cup dry white wine
¼ cup Cointreau
Fresh mint for garnish (optional)

1. With paring knife, peel orange, removing as much of the white pith as possible. Place orange on cutting surface and cut between each membrane to free segments. Rinse strawberries briefly in cool water and pat dry with paper towels. Hull them, if you wish.
2. Slice pineapple in half and then into quarters. Cut pineapple flesh from rind of 2 quarters. Reserve remaining 2 quarters for another use. Then cut flesh crosswise into 1-inch sections. Place on serving platter. Arrange strawberries and orange segments around pineapple.
3. In small bowl, combine sugar and wine. Drizzle mixture over fruit. Cover and refrigerate.
4. About 15 minutes before serving, remove fruit from refrigerator, add Cointreau, and toss gently.
5. Serve garnished with mint sprigs, if desired.

---

LEFTOVER SUGGESTION

To use up the leftover pineapple half at another meal, cut the flesh from the rind, cube it, then sprinkle the cubes with Kirsch, a dry clear brandy made from cherries and cherry pits.

# Oyster Pepper Pan Roast
# Beet and Endive Salad
# Hot Blueberry Betty

Fresh oysters are at their peak from early fall through spring, and are equally delicious raw or cooked, as in this recipe. Because they are delicate, they require gentle poaching just until their edges curl. Buy oysters, either in the shell or shucked, from your fish store. Packed in a tightly closed container in their natural juices, they will last for several days in the refrigerator. If you prefer a purer oyster flavor, omit the onion-pepper embellishments.

The Blueberry Betty, flavored with cinnamon and grated orange rind, calls for fresh blueberries. When these are not in season, use frozen, dry-packed blueberries rather than syrup-packed berries.

Remember, oysters cook very quickly; your guests should be seated before you begin to poach the oysters.

## WHAT TO DRINK

Choose a crisp, bone-dry wine and chill it well. First choice would be a French Muscadet; also very good would be a New York State Seyval Blanc.

## SHOPPING LIST AND STAPLES

2 dozen oysters in the shell or 1½ pints shucked
1 yellow onion

*Oyster pepper pan roast, in rimmed soup plates, makes a delicious main course. A textured salad of beets and endive, sprinkled with chopped parsley, and a crumb-topped blueberry dessert complete this company meal.*

4 small heads Belgian endive
1 green pepper
Small bunch parsley (optional)
1 quart fresh blueberries, preferably, or 3 ten-ounce
  packages frozen
1 lemon
1 orange (optional)
1 stick plus 4 tablespoons unsalted butter
1 quart vanilla ice cream (optional)
8¼-ounce can sliced beets
½ cup olive oil
2 tablespoons red wine vinegar
1 tablespoon Worcestershire sauce
4 slices home-style white bread
1 cup all-purpose flour

1 cup light brown sugar
2 tablespoons cornstarch
Dash of Cayenne pepper
Dash of nutmeg
1 teaspoon ground cinnamon
Salt and freshly ground pepper

## UTENSILS

Large heavy-gauge skillet
1½-quart casserole
2 large bowls
2 small bowls
Colander
Sieve

Measuring cups and spoons
Chef's knife
Paring knife
Metal spoon
Wooden spoon
Whisk
Grater or zester (optional)
Pastry blender (optional)
Flour sifter

## START-TO-FINISH STEPS

*In the morning:* If using frozen blueberries, transfer to refrigerator to thaw.

1. Grate orange rind, if using, and follow blueberry betty recipe steps 1 through 5.
2. While blueberry betty is baking, follow beet salad recipe steps 1 through 3. Chop parsley, if using, and set aside.
3. Mince onion and chop green pepper for oyster pepper pan roast. Shuck oysters, if necessary, drain, and follow oyster recipe steps 1 through 4.
4. Immediately after serving oysters, follow salad recipe step 4 and serve as an accompaniment.
5. For dessert, remove blueberry betty from oven, allow to cool slightly, and follow step 6.

## RECIPES

### Oyster Pepper Pan Roast

1 stick unsalted butter
¼ cup minced yellow onion
¼ cup chopped green pepper
4 slices home-style white bread
2 dozen oysters in the shell, or 1½ pints shucked and drained
1 tablespoon Worcestershire sauce
Dash of Cayenne pepper
Salt
Freshly ground pepper
1 lemon

1. In skillet, melt 3 tablespoons butter over medium heat. Add onion and green pepper, and sauté, stirring, 3 to 5 minutes, until softened.
2. While onion and green pepper are cooking, toast bread, then slice on diagonal. Halve lemon.

*Use oyster knife to pry open shell.*

3. Add remaining 5 tablespoons butter to skillet. When melted, add oysters, Worcestershire sauce, Cayenne pepper, salt and pepper to taste, and a squeeze of lemon juice. (Catch pits by holding sieve over skillet and squeezing lemon through it.) Stirring constantly, poach oysters over low heat 1 or 2 minutes, until they plump up and edges curl slightly.
4. Divide oysters, vegetables, and liquid among soup bowls. Place toast halves on rims of soup bowls. Serve at once.

### Beet and Endive Salad

8¼-ounce can sliced beets
4 small heads Belgian endive
2 tablespoons red wine vinegar
½ teaspoon salt
Freshly ground pepper
½ cup olive oil
1 tablespoon chopped parsley for garnish (optional)

1. Drain beets, stack, and dice. Place in salad bowl.
2. Wash and trim endive; discard ends. Slice endive crosswise into 1-inch pieces. Add to salad bowl and toss gently with beets. Cover and refrigerate until ready to serve.
3. In small bowl, blend vinegar, salt, and pepper to taste. Add olive oil in a slow, steady stream, whisking continuously until well combined. Set aside.
4. Stir dressing to recombine. Pour just enough dressing over salad to moisten it. Refrigerate remaining dressing for use another time. Toss salad and sprinkle with chopped parsley, if desired.

### Hot Blueberry Betty

1 quart fresh blueberries or 3 ten-ounce packages frozen, thawed
2 tablespoons cornstarch
1 teaspoon ground cinnamon
Dash of nutmeg
½ teaspoon grated orange rind (optional)
1 cup all-purpose flour
1 cup firmly packed light brown sugar
4 tablespoons butter
1 quart vanilla ice cream (optional)

1. Preheat oven to 375 degrees. Lightly butter casserole.
2. In colander, rinse blueberries under cool running water. Drain and pick over. Gently pat dry with paper towels and transfer to large bowl.
3. In small bowl, combine cornstarch, cinnamon, nutmeg, and orange rind, if desired. Pour over blueberries; toss well. Turn mixture into casserole. Wipe out bowl.
4. Sift flour and sugar together into bowl, add butter, and, with 2 knives or pastry blender, cut through mixture until it is crumbly. Sprinkle mixture over berries.
5. Bake 45 minutes.
6. Serve warm with vanilla ice cream, if desired.

# Pasta with Scallops, Ham, and Tongue
# Lettuce and Chicory Salad
# Glazed Fruits with Crème Fraîche

*Serve the pasta with scallops and julienned ham and tongue on individual dinner plates, with the mixed greens on the side.*

*Raspberries and sliced kiwi on crème fraîche (or whipped cream) add a brilliant splash of color.*

Scallops are prized for the delicately flavored muscle that controls their movements. In bay scallops, this muscle is pinkish-ivory and about half an inch in diameter. In sea scallops, it is beige, 2 inches or larger in diameter, and stronger in flavor. In either case, when fresh, scallops are translucent. Avoid any that are opaque, as this may indicate age or prior freezing. Since scallops cook rapidly, have all other ingredients for this recipe at hand before you begin to cook.

Purchase thick cuts of ham and tongue; if they are sliced too thin, you cannot cut them into a successful julienne, that is, into matchstick-size strips. If tongue is not available, you can omit it and double the ham.

The dessert calls for kiwi, also known as Chinese gooseberry, an oval, fuzzy brown fruit with lime-green, slightly tart flesh. If you cannot find kiwi, substitute figs. If raspberries are not available, use any other ripe fresh berries such as strawberries, suggested here. You can purchase crème fraîche at well-stocked supermarkets or specialty food stores, or make your own following the recipe on page 9.

## WHAT TO DRINK

A dry, full-bodied white wine would show off these rich flavors very nicely: a good California Chardonnay or a French Burgundy, such as a Meursault or Chassagne Montrachet.

## SHOPPING LIST AND STAPLES

¼ pound cooked ham, in ½-inch-thick slices
¼ pound cooked tongue, in ½-inch-thick slices
1 pound bay or sea scallops
1 head Boston lettuce
1 head chicory, or escarole
1 lemon
Small bunch parsley (optional)
Small bunch mint (optional)
½ pint fresh raspberries or strawberries
4 ripe kiwi or fresh figs
7 tablespoons unsalted butter
½ pint crème fraîche, preferably homemade (see page 9), or commercial, or heavy cream
½ cup olive oil
2 tablespoons vegetable oil

2 tablespoons red wine vinegar
10-ounce jar red currant jelly
1 teaspoon Dijon mustard
1 pound linguine or spaghetti, preferably fresh whole wheat, or dried
1 cup flour (approximately)
1 tablespoon sugar
Salt and freshly ground pepper

## UTENSILS

Stockpot or kettle
Small skillet
Small saucepan
10-inch heavy-gauge sauté pan
Heatproof serving platter
2 large bowls, plus 1 additional (if using heavy cream)
2 small bowls
Colander
Measuring cups and spoons
Chef's knife
Paring knife
Slotted spoon
2 wooden spoons
Rubber spatula
Whisk
Electric mixer (optional)
Salad spinner (optional)

## START-TO-FINISH STEPS

1. If using heavy cream in glazed fruits recipe, chill mixing bowl and beaters or whisk. Follow salad recipe steps 1 and 2.
2. Follow glazed fruits recipe steps 1 and 2.
3. Chop parsley, julienne ham and tongue, and follow scallops and pasta recipe steps 1 through 9.
4. Follow salad recipe step 3 and serve with the pasta.
5. For dessert, follow glazed fruit recipe steps 3 through 5.

## RECIPES

### Pasta with Scallops, Ham, and Tongue

1 pound bay or sea scallops
4 tablespoons unsalted butter, plus 3 tablespoons (optional)

¾ cup cooked, sliced ham (about ¼ pound), cut into julienne strips, 1 by ½ inch
¾ cup cooked, sliced beef tongue (about ¼ pound), cut into julienne strips, 1 by ½ inch
1 pound linguine or spaghetti, preferably fresh whole wheat, or dried
1 cup flour for dredging (approximately)
2 tablespoons vegetable oil
Salt
Freshly ground pepper
1 lemon, halved
¼ cup chopped parsley for garnish (optional)

1. Preheat oven to 200 degrees.
2. In stockpot or kettle, bring 4 quarts water to a boil.
3. Place serving platter and large bowl in preheated oven to warm.
4. Wipe scallops dry with paper towels and, if using sea scallops, halve them. Set aside.
5. In small skillet, melt 2 tablespoons butter over medium heat. Add ham and tongue, and cook, stirring, until warmed through. Transfer meat to warm bowl and return to oven.
6. When water has come to a boil, add pasta and stir to separate strands. Cook until pasta is *al dente*—barely tender but still firm. Fresh pasta will cook in approximately 5 to 7 minutes, dried pasta in 10 to 12 minutes. Drain in colander.
7. Add cooked pasta to ham and tongue, and toss gently to combine. Turn onto warm serving platter and return to oven.
8. Place about 1 cup flour on sheet of wax paper. Dredge scallops; shake off excess flour. In 10-inch heavy-gauge sauté pan, heat vegetable oil and 2 tablespoons butter over high heat. When oil is hot, add scallops and sauté quickly 3 to 4 minutes, until pale gold. Do not crowd pan, and be careful not to overcook. Season with salt, pepper, and lemon juice to taste.
9. With slotted spoon, remove scallops and arrange over pasta. Serve garnished with parsley, if desired. Or, before adding parsley, you can prepare a quick brown-butter sauce: Pour off any excess fat from sauté pan and add remaining 3 tablespoons butter. Cook over medium-high heat until butter turns golden brown, about 2 to 3 minutes. Pour the brown butter sauce over the scallops and pasta, then garnish with chopped parsley, if desired, and serve immediately.

## Lettuce and Chicory Salad

1 head Boston lettuce
1 head chicory or escarole
2 tablespoons red wine vinegar
½ teaspoon salt
Freshly ground black pepper
1 teaspoon Dijon mustard
½ cup olive oil

1. Wash lettuce and chicory. Spin dry in salad spinner or pat dry with paper towels. Wrap in kitchen towel and refrigerate.
2. In small bowl, combine vinegar, salt, and pepper to taste. Whisk in mustard. Add oil in a slow, steady stream, whisking continuously, until dressing is thick and smooth.
3. Put lettuce in salad bowl and toss with enough dressing just to coat lightly. Reserve remaining dressing in refrigerator for future use.

## Glazed Fruits with Crème Fraîche

1 cup crème fraîche or heavy cream
½ pint fresh raspberries or strawberries
4 ripe kiwi or fresh figs
½ cup red currant jelly
1 tablespoon sugar
Fresh mint leaves for garnish (optional)

1. If using heavy cream, beat with hand mixer or whisk in large bowl until soft peaks form. Be careful not to overbeat. Refrigerate until ready to use.
2. In colander, rinse raspberries or strawberries briefly under cool running water and drain. Gently pat dry with paper towels. If using strawberries, slice large ones in half. Cover fruit loosely and refrigerate. Peel each kiwi and slice vertically into quarters, just to the base, so that quarters remain attached at bottom. If using figs, do not peel, but slice as you would kiwi.
3. Using rubber spatula, make a bed of crème fraîche or whipped cream in center of each dessert plate. Set a peeled and sliced kiwi in center of each plate, gently open it, and in center of kiwi, mound berries.
4. In saucepan, combine currant jelly and sugar. Cook over moderately high heat 2 to 3 minutes, until jelly has melted enough to thickly coat a wooden spoon. Remove from heat and cool slightly.
5. Drizzle glaze over berries. Garnish with mint leaves, if desired.

# Maria Robbins

MENU 1 (Left)
**Fruit Crudités with Roquefort Cheese Spread
Ham Dumplings with Fried Onions
and Mushrooms
Watercress and Grapefruit Salad**

MENU 2
**Asparagus with Prosciutto
Russian Farmer Cheese Pancakes with Sugared
Strawberries and Sour Cream
Carrot-Apple Salad**

MENU 3
**Sliced Oranges and Bananas
Baked Potatoes Topped with
Sautéed Chicken Livers
Sautéed Cherry Tomatoes
French Bread Toasted with Parmesan Cheese**

M aria Robbins singles out her Russian herit-
age as the major influence on her cooking. As
a child, she lived in an emigré community in
New York, surrounded by dedicated Old
Country cooks, including her mother and her aunt. Maria
Robbins remembers, "We had come to America having
survived the disruption, violence, and deprivations of
World War II. Memories of famine and starvation, food
shortages, and years of making do were the stimuli for the
endless hours of preparing rich, comforting food." Such a
background teaches respect for ingredients and cultivates
a memory for taste that guides more accurately than any
recipe, she feels.

Most of her favorite dishes originated in peasant kitchens: stews, soups, and filled dumplings. Each menu bears
the stamp of her past. Dumplings in various guises are a
popular Russian food, and the main course of Menu 1 is
dumplings made with ham and ricotta cheese, and topped
with fried mushrooms and onions. The highlight of Menu 2
is the Russian farmer cheese pancakes, resembling the
traditional *Syrniki*—sweetened cheese pancakes. As a
Russian cook would, Maria Robbins rolls the thick dough
into a sausage or cylinder shape, then chills it so it will firm
before cooking. Potatoes topped with sautéed chicken
livers and a sour-cream sherry sauce is the ample main
course for Menu 3.

*The Roquefort cheese spread, crunchy with chopped nuts,
accompanies raw, unpeeled apple and pear slices. Follow
this first course with warm ham dumplings and the tossed
watercress and grapefruit salad. A bowl of fruit is a
compatible centerpiece here.*

# Fruit Crudités with Roquefort Cheese Spread
# Ham Dumplings with Fried Onions and Mushrooms
# Watercress and Grapefruit Salad

The French term "crudités" generally refers to an assortment of cut-up raw vegetables or fruit presented as an hors d'oeuvre. For this brunch, the first course is a fruit crudité platter that consists of sliced apples and pears, accompanied by a Roquefort cheese spread. Blue-veined Roquefort, made from sheep's milk in the French village of Roquefort-Sur-Soulzon, has a sharp flavor. Less costly blue cheeses, imported or domestic, resemble the French Roquefort in taste and texture and can be used instead.

Day-old bread, cut into cubes then soaked in a milk and egg mixture, becomes the basic dough for the dumplings. Ground ham, eggs, parsley, and seasonings make the dumplings rich and savory, and ricotta cheese combines with them to create a smooth texture. As they cook, dumplings expand because steam forms within the dough. To provide ample room for expansion, always cook dumplings in a large stockpot and never crowd them. Because dumpling dough is fragile, the cooking water must simmer rather than boil. Remove each dumpling from the pot when it is firm and a cake tester inserted in the center comes out clean.

Watercress should have fresh crisp leaves, with no signs of wilting or yellowing. Store it in a plastic bag in the vegetable crisper of your refrigerator and wash just before using. It will keep for up to one week.

## WHAT TO DRINK

To accompany the medley of flavors in this menu, serve a light red wine, such as a French Beaujolais or California Gamay.

## SHOPPING LIST AND STAPLES

¾ pound cooked ham
Small head red cabbage
2 medium-size onions
¼ pound mushrooms
Small head lettuce (optional)
1 bunch watercress
1 bunch parsley
1 seedless grapefruit
2 large Red Delicious apples
2 large ripe pears
3 eggs
1 stick plus 4 tablespoons unsalted butter
1 cup milk

8-ounce container sour cream
¼ pound Roquefort cheese
8-ounce container ricotta cheese
3 tablespoons safflower oil
8 slices day-old bread (approximately)
4-ounce can pecans or walnuts
½ cup flour (approximately)
¼ teaspoon sugar
Salt and freshly ground pepper

## UTENSILS

Food processor or meat grinder
Blender (if not using food processor)
Stockpot or kettle
Medium-size heavy skillet
Ovenproof dish
Salad bowl
Large bowl (if not using food processor)
Medium-size bowl
Small bowl
Measuring cups and spoons
Chef's knife
Paring knife
Wooden spoon
Slotted spoon
Metal spatula
Grater (if not using food processor)
Serrated grapefruit knife

## START-TO-FINISH STEPS

1. Follow dumplings recipe step 1. While water is coming to a boil, make bread crumbs for onion-mushroom topping, and cut bread for dumplings into ½-inch cubes. Chop parsley for dumplings and topping.
2. Follow crudités recipe step 1 and prepare lettuce for garnish, if desired.
3. Follow salad recipe steps 1 through 3.
4. Follow dumplings recipe steps 2 through 7.
5. While dumplings are cooking, follow topping recipe steps 1 through 5 and crudités recipe step 2.
6. Cover dumplings loosely with aluminum foil, and keep warm in oven.
7. Serve crudités.
8. Follow salad recipe step 4 and dumplings recipe step 8. Serve together.

## Fruit Crudités with Roquefort Cheese Spread

¼ pound Roquefort cheese
½ cup sour cream
½ cup chopped pecans or walnuts plus ¼ cup for garnish
  (optional)
2 large Red Delicious apples
2 large ripe pears
Lettuce leaves for garnish (optional)

1. In medium-size bowl, mash Roquefort with fork. Stir in sour cream and chopped nuts. Cover until ready to use.
2. Just before serving, quarter and core apples and pears. Do not peel. Cut each quarter into 3 or 4 slices. Arrange fruit slices and cheese spread on lettuce-lined plate and garnish with chopped nuts, if desired.

## Ham Dumplings with Fried Onions and Mushrooms

Salt
1 stick unsalted butter
3 cups ½-inch cubes day-old bread
¼ to ½ cup milk
¾ pound cooked ham
3 eggs
½ cup ricotta cheese
½ cup coarsely chopped parsley
Freshly ground pepper
½ cup flour (approximately)
Onion-mushroom topping (see following recipe)

1. In stockpot or kettle, bring 4 quarts salted water to a simmer.
2. Melt butter in skillet. Add bread cubes and toss with spatula until they absorb butter. Turn off heat and add milk. Continue tossing bread cubes until they have absorbed all the milk.
3. Grind ham in food processor fitted with metal blade or in meat grinder. If using food processor, add bread cubes, eggs, ricotta cheese, parsley, salt, and pepper. Process until combined. Or, in large bowl, combine all ingredients thoroughly. Knead mixture with your hands until it is almost doughlike and holds together.
4. Sprinkle flour on a sheet of wax paper. Dust hands with flour and form ham mixture into 1½-inch balls, coating each one with flour. Set balls on second sheet of wax paper.
5. Preheat oven to 200 degrees.
6. With slotted spoon, add dumplings to simmering water, a few at a time. Be careful not to crowd them. Poach at a gentle simmer 10 minutes after they float to the top.
7. As they are done, remove dumplings with slotted spoon to heatproof platter and keep warm in oven while you cook remaining dumplings.
8. Just before serving, spoon dumplings onto individual plates and spread onion-mushroom topping over each portion.

## Onion-Mushroom Topping

4 tablespoons unsalted butter
2 medium-size onions
¼ pound mushrooms
1 cup fresh, unseasoned bread crumbs
½ cup chopped parsley
Salt
Freshly ground pepper

1. Melt butter in skillet used for dumpling recipe.
2. Using chef's knife, chop onions finely and add to butter. Cook over low heat, stirring occasionally with wooden spoon, until golden brown, about 15 minutes.
3. While onions are cooking, clean mushrooms with damp paper towel. Using chef's knife, trim and finely chop mushrooms. Add them to onions. Cook, stirring with wooden spoon, 1 minute, then add bread crumbs.
4. Continue to cook, stirring, until bread crumbs are browned.
5. Add parsley, salt, and pepper. Remove from heat. Cover and keep warm in oven until ready to serve.

## Watercress and Grapefruit Salad

¼ small head red cabbage
1 bunch watercress
1 seedless grapefruit
3 tablespoons safflower oil
¼ teaspoon sugar
Salt
Freshly ground pepper

1. Using food processor or coarse side of grater, shred cabbage and put in salad bowl.
2. Rinse and dry watercress. Remove stems, if desired, and break watercress into sprigs. Add to salad bowl.
3. Peel grapefruit, removing all the white pith (see diagram below). Holding the peeled grapefruit over salad bowl to catch juice, cut with sharp paring knife between section membranes and let sections fall into bowl. Refrigerate until ready to serve.
4. Into small bowl, squeeze remaining membranes to remove any juice. Discard membranes. Add oil, sugar, and salt and pepper to taste. Mix well, pour over salad, and toss.

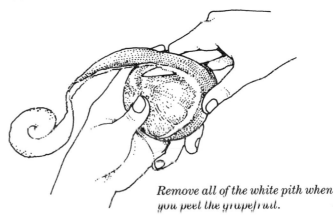

*Remove all of the white pith when you peel the grapefruit.*

# Asparagus with Prosciutto
# Russian Farmer Cheese Pancakes with Sugared Strawberries and Sour Cream
# Carrot-Apple Salad

*Serve the elegant prosciutto-wrapped asparagus as a first course. The pancakes, topped with sugared strawberries, look attractive on a large platter. Serve cups of hot* café au lait, *if you wish, to complete the meal.*

In this spring brunch the appetizer is asparagus spears bundled in prosciutto. This Italian air-cured unsmoked ham has a spicy assertive taste and, at its best, is moist and pink. It should not be sliced paper thin because it becomes too fragile. If you cannot find prosciutto, use thinly sliced boiled ham. Select asparagus that are plump, bright green, smooth skinned, and have compact tips. Open leafy tips are sure signs of age. Round thick spears are usually more tender than thin or flat ones. Before storing the asparagus, cut off a small piece from the bottom of each spear, then stand them upright in a container of cold water in the refrigerator. The asparagus should stay fresh for several days.

Maria Robbins's Russian pancakes call for farmer cheese, a granular, firm, bland cheese made from cultured milk. Higher in fat content and drier than cottage cheese, which it resembles, farmer cheese is commonly sold pressed into blocks for easy slicing.

The grated carrot and apple salad provides a refreshing taste and texture contrast to the pancakes. For extra color, leave the apples unpeeled. Yogurt and lemon juice add a tart flavor, mellowed by a little honey.

## WHAT TO DRINK

Asparagus does not go well with any wine, but in this case, the presence of prosciutto helps balance the flavor so that a lightly sweet wine can be used. First choice would be a good German Kabinett or Spätlese.

## SHOPPING LIST AND STAPLES

8 very thin slices prosciutto (about ¼ pound total weight)
20 to 24 asparagus spears (about 1½ pounds)
1 pound carrots
1 pint fresh ripe strawberries, preferably, or 10-ounce package frozen, unsweetened
2 large Granny Smith or Red Delicious apples
1 lemon
2 eggs
1 pint sour cream
3 tablespoons unsalted butter
1 pound farmer cheese
8-ounce container plain yogurt
⅓ cup plus 3 tablespoons flour
3 tablespoons sugar
1 tablespoon honey

Salt
Freshly ground pepper

## UTENSILS

Food processor (if not using grater)
Oval casserole or deep skillet
Nonstick skillet
Heatproof platter
3 medium-size bowls
Small bowl
Colander or strainer
Measuring cups and spoons
Chef's knife
Paring knife
Wooden spoons
Spatula
Grater
Citrus juicer
Tongs

## START-TO-FINISH STEPS

1. Follow pancakes recipe steps 1 and 2.
2. While pancake mixture is chilling, follow carrot-apple salad recipe steps 1 through 4.
3. Follow asparagus recipe steps 1 through 3.
4. While asparagus cooks, follow strawberries recipe steps 1 and 2.
5. Follow asparagus recipe step 4.
6. Follow pancakes recipe steps 3 through 5. Keep warm in oven while serving asparagus.
7. Turn sour cream into serving bowl and follow pancakes recipe step 6. Serve with the carrot-apple salad.

## RECIPES

### Asparagus with Prosciutto

20 to 24 asparagus spears (about 1½ pounds)
1 tablespoon salt
Juice of ½ lemon
8 very thin slices prosciutto (about ¼ pound total weight)
Freshly ground black pepper (optional)

1. Bring ½ inch water to a boil in oval casserole or deep skillet.

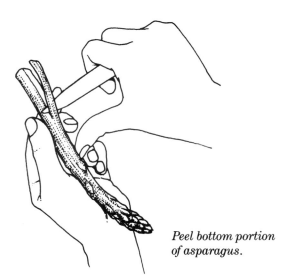

*Peel bottom portion of asparagus.*

**2.** Using paring knife, trim asparagus spears to remove tough ends. Peel stalks and rinse them under cold water.
**3.** Add salt to boiling water, then add asparagus. Simmer, covered, just until tender. Cooking time will vary according to size of asparagus. If spears are very thin, start testing at 4 minutes. Thicker spears may require 10 minutes or more. With tongs, remove asparagus to plate lined with paper towels and let cool.
**4.** Sprinkle asparagus with lemon juice and divide into 4 portions. Wrap each portion in 2 slices of prosciutto. Grate pepper over prosciutto, if desired.

## Russian Farmer Cheese Pancakes with Sugared Strawberries and Sour Cream

2 eggs
1 pound farmer cheese
⅓ cup flour plus 3 tablespoons for dredging
1 tablespoon sugar
Pinch of salt
2 to 3 tablespoons unsalted butter (approximately)
Sugared strawberries (see following recipe)
1 pint sour cream

**1.** Separate eggs, reserving whites for another use. In medium-size bowl, combine farmer cheese, egg yolks, ⅓ cup flour, sugar, and salt; with wooden spoon, mix until well blended.
**2.** Place mixture on sheet of wax paper and roll into sausage shape about 12 inches long and 2 inches in diameter. Wrap in wax paper and chill in freezer 20 to 30 minutes.

**3.** Preheat oven to 200 degrees. Remove pancake roll from freezer, unwrap, and score at 1-inch intervals to make 12 portions. Slice through with chef's knife. Shape slightly to make rounds or ovals about ½ inch thick. Spread 3 tablespoons flour on wax paper and lightly dredge pancakes, shaking off any excess flour. Warm heatproof platter in oven.
**4.** In nonstick skillet, melt 2 tablespoons butter.
**5.** Fry a few pancakes at a time—do not let them touch each other. Cook over medium heat until golden brown on each side, about 2 minutes on first side, slightly less on the second. Add more butter as necessary. Remove pancakes with spatula, place on preheated platter, and keep warm in oven as you cook the remaining pancakes.
**6.** Serve pancakes with sugared strawberries and sour cream.

## Sugared Strawberries

1 pint fresh ripe strawberries, preferably, or 10-ounce package frozen, unsweetened
2 to 3 tablespoons sugar

**1.** Hull berries and lightly rinse in strainer or colander. Pat dry with paper towels. If using frozen berries, thaw in wrapping in bowl of warm water.
**2.** Halve strawberries, place in medium-size bowl, and toss with sugar to taste. Set aside until ready to serve.

## Carrot-Apple Salad

1 pound carrots
2 large Granny Smith or Red Delicious apples
1 tablespoon lemon juice
1 tablespoon honey
1 cup plain yogurt

**1.** Trim and peel carrots. Using grater or food processor fitted with shredding disk, grate carrots. Place in medium-size bowl.
**2.** With paring knife, quarter and core apples. Peel them, if desired. Grate apples and add to carrots. Toss to combine.
**3.** In small bowl, combine lemon juice and honey. Pour over apple-carrot mixture. Toss gently, add yogurt, and toss once more. Divide salad among individual serving bowls.
**4.** Refrigerate until ready to serve.

# Sliced Oranges and Bananas
# Baked Potatoes Topped with Sautéed Chicken Livers
# Sautéed Cherry Tomatoes/French Bread Toasted with Parmesan Cheese

*Sautéed cherry tomatoes are a perfect accompaniment for baked potatoes topped with chicken livers and cheese-sprinkled*

*French bread. For a decorative garnish, arrange sliced mushrooms and cherry tomatoes on dill*

For the light fruit salad served before the baked potato entrée, buy large seedless navel oranges, which are the easiest to peel. Select firm, hefty oranges with bright, smooth skins. A rough-textured skin may mean the orange is dry. At a cool room temperature or in the refrigerator, oranges will last up to two weeks.

Idaho potatoes have dry, mealy insides that become fluffy when baked. Select firm well-shaped potatoes of a uniform size and without any sprouts or bitter-tasting green spots. Stored in a cool, dry place, they should keep for several months.

Buy chicken livers that are plump, moist, odor-free, and deep red, without any discolorations. Before you cook the livers, trim away any tough connecting tissues.

## WHAT TO DRINK

The rich chicken livers need a full-bodied white or red wine to accompany them. For white, try a California Chardonnay; for red, a California Barbera.

## SHOPPING LIST AND STAPLES

1 pound chicken livers
4 Idaho baking potatoes
1 medium-size onion
¼ pound mushrooms
1 pint cherry tomatoes
Small bunch scallions
Small bunch dill (optional)
2 oranges
2 bananas
1 pint sour cream
6 tablespoons unsalted butter
¼ pound Parmesan cheese
3 tablespoons vegetable oil
¼ teaspoon vanilla extract
1 loaf French bread
1 tablespoon flour
2 tablespoons brown sugar
Salt
Freshly ground black pepper
½ cup dry sherry

## UTENSILS

Wok or skillet
Large skillet

Large bowl
Medium-size bowl
Small bowl
Colander
Measuring cups and spoons
Chef's knife
Paring knife
Wooden spoons
Wooden spatula
Cheese grater
Vegetable brush
Darning needle

## START-TO-FINISH STEPS

**1.** Follow baked potatoes recipe steps 1 through 3.
**2.** While potatoes are baking, follow oranges and bananas recipe steps 1 through 4.
**3.** Follow chicken livers recipe steps 1 through 5.
**4.** Follow cherry tomatoes recipe step 1.
**5.** Follow bread recipe steps 1 and 2.
**6.** Follow sliced oranges and bananas recipe step 5.
**7.** Follow chicken livers recipe step 6.
**8.** Follow bread recipe step 3 and cherry tomatoes recipe step 2.
**9.** Remove potatoes from oven and follow potatoes recipe steps 4 through 6.
**10.** Remove bread from oven and serve with the stuffed potatoes and tomatoes.

## RECIPES

### Sliced Oranges and Bananas

¼ teaspoon vanilla extract
2 tablespoons brown sugar
½ cup sour cream
2 oranges
2 bananas

**1.** In a medium-size bowl, combine vanilla extract, brown sugar, and sour cream.
**2.** Peel oranges. Remove as much of the pith as possible. Using paring knife, cut along membrane on either side of each orange segment (see following diagram). Pull segments apart and halve them, if desired.
**3.** Peel bananas and slice into large bowl.

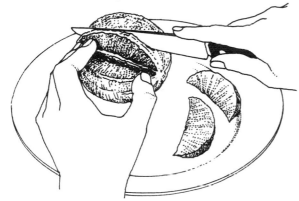

*Cut between membranes to segment orange.*

4. Add oranges and sour cream mixture, and toss gently to combine. Refrigerate until ready to serve.
5. Serve in individual bowls, goblets, or sherbet glasses.

## Baked Potatoes Topped with Sautéed Chicken Livers

4 Idaho baking potatoes
2 tablespoons vegetable oil
2 to 3 scallions
Sautéed chicken livers (see following recipe)
2 to 3 tablespoons chopped dill for garnish (optional)

1. Preheat oven to 425 degrees.
2. Scrub potatoes and pat dry. Rub lightly with vegetable oil. Pierce with fork in several places and place them on middle rack of oven. Bake 50 minutes, or until done.
3. Trim off scallion roots and any discolored tops. Chop scallions, including green tops.
4. Using knife, split potatoes lengthwise. Press down on flesh with fork and mash slightly.
5. Spoon sautéed chicken livers into potato cavities.
6. Sprinkle with chopped scallions and dill, if desired.

## Sautéed Chicken Livers

1 pound chicken livers
Salt
Freshly ground black pepper
1 tablespoon flour
¼ pound mushrooms
4 tablespoons unsalted butter
1 medium-size onion
½ cup dry sherry
3 to 4 tablespoons sour cream (optional)

1. Wash the chicken livers and cut away membranes and any dark spots with paring knife. Pat dry with paper towels.
2. On sheet of wax paper, combine ¼ teaspoon salt, pepper to taste, and flour. Lightly dredge chicken livers, turning to coat evenly.
3. Clean mushrooms with damp paper towel and then slice.
4. In large skillet, melt butter. While it is melting, peel onion and cut into fine dice. Add to skillet and cook over medium heat, stirring, until soft and translucent, 2 to 3 minutes.
5. Add mushrooms and cook, stirring, until they soften, about 3 to 5 minutes.
6. Add chicken livers and sauté 3 or 4 minutes, until they turn brown but are still slightly pink in center. Cut into one to test for doneness. Add sherry and cook 1 minute at high heat, until sauce is thick and slightly reduced. Remove from heat and stir in sour cream, if desired; add salt and pepper to taste.

## Sautéed Cherry Tomatoes

1 pint cherry tomatoes
1 tablespoon vegetable oil
Salt
Freshly ground black pepper

1. Pick over tomatoes, remove stems, rinse, and drain in colander. Prick stem end of each tomato with darning needle to prevent tomato from bursting while cooking.
2. In skillet or wok, heat oil until hot and add tomatoes. Using 2 wooden spoons, toss tomatoes in oil and sauté about 3 minutes. Season with salt and pepper to taste.

## French Bread Toasted With Parmesan Cheese

½ cup freshly grated Parmesan cheese
2 tablespoons unsalted butter, at room temperature
1 loaf French bread

1. Using wooden spoon, mash cheese with butter in small bowl to form a paste.
2. Split bread lengthwise and spread cheese-butter mixture on both sides. Score bread crosswise, marking large pieces for easy serving. Wrap in aluminum foil, leaving top open so cheese will brown.
3. Place bread in 425-degree oven and bake 10 to 12 minutes, or until browned.

# Diane Darrow and Tom Maresca

### MENU 1 (Right)
Quick Sage Bread
Poached Eggs with Red Wine Sauce
Grapefruit Compote

### MENU 2
Slab Bacon Roasted on Red and White Beans
Baked Green Peppers
Sweet Pear Breads

### MENU 3
Smoked Sable and Salmon Rolls with
Cream Cheese and Caviar
Chicken Breasts Béarnaise
Leaf Lettuce and Mushroom Salad
Broiled Peach Halves with Raspberry Jam

D iane Darrow and Tom Maresca favor noontime brunches that stretch until dinnertime. Their brunches are substantial meals, complete with proteins, carbohydrates, and fresh produce. They serve small courses—often their own adaptations of more classic fare—in sequence rather than an entire meal at one time. For example, in the first course in Menu 3, two moderately priced caviars and cream cheese blend with smoked sable and smoked salmon in a dish reminiscent of a popular New York breakfast, lox (salt-cured salmon) and bagels; in the second, sautéed chicken breasts with a béarnaise sauce is an interesting variation of eggs Benedict; and, in the last course, peaches with raspberry jam are a simplified version of peach Melba, peaches filled with vanilla ice cream and topped with raspberry purée.

Their other two menus show how they turn brunch into the nutritional focal point of a leisurely Sunday. In Menu 1, poached eggs in a red wine and bacon sauce, served on toast, is a delicately flavored, filling dish, complemented by sage bread and a grapefruit compote. Menu 2 features cold-weather fare, an old-fashioned meal of beans baked with bacon, followed by sweet pear breads, an adaptation of an Italian dessert. Baked green peppers, another Italian-style dish, provide both color and texture contrast to the main dish.

*Poached eggs on toast, with a red wine sauce and crumbled bacon, are the basis of an easy but elegant company brunch. Squares of freshly baked sage bread, arranged in a bread basket or on a serving plate, and a grapefruit and prune compote, brightened with slivers of lemon peel, can be served separately.*

# Quick Sage Bread
# Poached Eggs with Red Wine Sauce
# Grapefruit Compote

The fresh, light compote includes grapefruit and steamed prunes, flavored with grated lemon peel and apricot brandy. The cooks suggest that you use Barack Pálinka, a dry, unsweetened apricot brandy from Hungary. If this is unavailable, a dry peach or plum brandy will do. Steaming plumps the prunes, but soaking them in boiling water 10 minutes works just as well. Drain the water before you add the prunes to the grapefruit. For a sweet compote, add sugar to taste. Before serving, macerate—or steep—the fruits in the brandy 15 minutes. This gives the fruit time to absorb the apricot flavor.

For their poached eggs in red wine sauce, the cooks prefer poaching the eggs in advance, cutting down on last-minute preparation time. Despite their delicacy, poached eggs will keep well for up to a day in a bowl of water in the refrigerator. They reheat without toughening, provided you warm them no longer than 1 minute. Of course, if you wish, you can poach them just before serving.

Since the eggs are served on toast, you may prefer to serve the sage bread either as a first course or with the fruit compote. Fresh sage imparts a more assertive flavor, but dried sage leaves are a satisfactory substitute for this savory quick bread.

## WHAT TO DRINK

A well-chilled white wine with good body and acid would complement the delicate flavors and tang of these dishes: a good California Sauvignon Blanc or French Chablis. If you prefer red wine, try a lightly chilled Beaujolais or a Loire red such as Chinon.

## SHOPPING LIST AND STAPLES

¼ pound lean bacon
4 medium-size grapefruit
1 lemon
Small onion
1 clove garlic
Small bunch parsley (optional)
1 tablespoon fresh sage leaves, or 1 teaspoon dried
12 to 18 prunes, preferably good quality (sold in bulk)
9 eggs
1 cup milk
9 tablespoons unsalted butter
½ cup chicken stock, preferably homemade (see page 13), or canned

2 tablespoons distilled white vinegar
4 to 8 slices firm white bread
1 cup plus 2 tablespoons flour
1 cup yellow cornmeal
6 tablespoons plus ½ teaspoon sugar
4 teaspoons baking powder
2 whole cloves
Bouquet garni (see page 14)
Salt
Freshly ground pepper
2 cups dry red wine
3 tablespoons apricot brandy, preferably Barack Pálinka

## UTENSILS

Large, deep skillet
Medium-size skillet with cover
Small skillet
Medium-size saucepan with cover
Small saucepan
Steamer
Kettle
8-by-8-inch baking dish
2 large bowls
Strainer
Measuring cups and spoons
Chef's knife
Paring knife
Slotted spoon
Wooden spoons
Rubber spatula
Grater
Whisk
Vegetable peeler
Straight pin or small needle
Toaster

## START-TO-FINISH STEPS

1. For sage bread, mince fresh sage or crumble dried and follow recipe steps 1 through 5.
2. While sage bread is baking, chop bacon and onion, and mince garlic for red wine sauce. Then follow recipe steps 1 and 2.
3. While red wine sauce is cooking, follow grapefruit recipe steps 1 and 2.

4. While grapefruit is macerating, follow poached eggs recipe, steps 1 through 4. (Eggs can be prepared as much as a day in advance and refrigerated, covered, in bowl of water.)

5. Follow red wine sauce recipe steps 3 through 6.

6. Follow sage bread recipe step 6.

7. Follow red wine sauce recipe step 7.

8. Serve sage bread and poached eggs, followed by compote.

---

RECIPES

## Quick Sage Bread

2 tablespoons butter
1 cup all-purpose flour
1 cup yellow cornmeal
6 tablespoons sugar
4 teaspoons baking powder
½ teaspoon salt
1 tablespoon minced fresh sage leaves, or 1 teaspoon crumbled dried
1 cup milk
1 egg, beaten

1. Preheat oven to 400 degrees.

2. In small saucepan, melt butter and cool.

3. In large bowl, stir together flour, cornmeal, sugar, baking powder, and salt. Stir in sage leaves. Combine milk, egg, and melted butter. Add to dry ingredients, stirring with wooden spoon just to a smooth consistency.

4. Grease 8-by-8-inch baking dish. Pour in sage batter and smooth with rubber spatula.

5. Bake 25 to 30 minutes, or until toothpick inserted near center comes out clean.

6. Remove bread from oven, let cool for a few minutes and cut into squares. Transfer to serving plate or bread basket and serve warm or at room temperature.

## Poached Eggs with Red Wine Sauce

6 tablespoons butter
½ cup plus 2 tablespoons coarsely chopped bacon
⅓ cup chopped onion
1 clove garlic, minced
2 whole cloves
2 cups dry red wine
½ teaspoon sugar
Salt
Freshly ground pepper
Bouquet garni
½ cup chicken stock, preferably homemade (see page 13), or canned
2 tablespoons flour
4 to 8 slices firm white bread
8 poached eggs (see following recipe)
Parsley sprigs (optional)

1. Heat 4 tablespoons butter in medium-size skillet and sauté ½ cup bacon, onion, and garlic until onion is soft and golden. In small skillet, cook remaining 2 tablespoons bacon. Drain on paper towels.

2. To skillet containing bacon and onion mixture, add whole cloves, wine, sugar, salt and pepper to taste, bouquet garni, and chicken stock. Simmer gently, covered, for 20 to 25 minutes.

3. With your fingers, rub together remaining 2 tablespoons butter and the flour to make a *beurre manié*, or thick paste. Roll into balls the size of grapes and set aside.

4. Strain sauce to remove bits of onion, bacon, and bouquet garni. Return sauce to skillet. Then thicken sauce with *beurre manié*: Bring sauce to a slow boil; add *beurre manié* balls; and, with whisk, beat constantly 1 minute or until sauce thickens. Taste sauce—if you detect a raw flour taste, cook another half minute or so.

5. When sauce is nearly done, toast bread slices.

6. Reheat poached eggs, step 5 of poached egg recipe.

7. Place poached eggs on toast, spoon sauce over them, and garnish with reserved bacon and, if desired, parsley sprigs. Serve at once.

## Poached Eggs

8 large eggs
1 to 2 tablespoons distilled white vinegar

1. In large, deep skillet, bring 2 inches of water to a boil. Pierce one end of each eggshell with straight pin or small needle. Gently place eggs in boiling water 10 seconds, then remove with slotted spoon.

2. Add vinegar to water and bring to a strong simmer. Have large bowl of ice water ready to "set" cooked eggs.

3. Gently break eggs into simmering water, one at a time, at intervals of about 15 seconds. Regulate heat so water barely simmers. Gently prod eggs after first few seconds to be sure they are floating free and not sticking to bottom of pan.

4. After 3½ minutes, remove eggs with slotted spoon. Immediately immerse in ice water to stop cooking. Leave in water till ready to proceed.

5. When ready, bring kettle of water to a boil. Drain cold water from bowl and gently pour boiling water around and over eggs to cover them completely. Leave eggs in hot water 1 minute, then drain them.

## Grapefruit Compote

12 to 18 medium-size dried prunes
4 medium-size grapefruit
1 lemon
3 tablespoons apricot brandy, preferably Barack Pálinka

1. In collapsible steamer fitted into medium-size saucepan, steam prunes, covered, 10 minutes. Remove and pit. Halve, if desired.

2. Peel and section grapefruit, taking care to remove pith and membranes. Put grapefruit sections in serving bowl. Grate lemon rind. Add rind, prunes, and apricot brandy to grapefruit. Stir gently and let macerate in refrigerator at least 15 minutes before serving.

# Slab Bacon Roasted on Red and White Beans
# Baked Green Peppers
# Sweet Pear Breads

As they bake, the red kidney beans and the cannellini (the Italian name for white kidney beans) absorb the sweet, tart, spicy flavors of the other ingredients in the casserole. Drain and rinse the beans before cooking to remove any metallic can taste. Deeply score the slab bacon so it cooks through completely. Smokehouse-style slab bacon, available at most meat markets, has a mild, smoky taste and is preferable to regular, packaged sliced bacon for this recipe.

Mild, sweetish Italian frying peppers are sold in most supermarkets. Because they are too fleshy, bell peppers would not be a suitable substitute for this recipe.

The ripe fruit in the sweet pear breads serves as a leavening agent; no baking powder or baking soda is needed. Use juicy pears, such as Anjou, Bartlett, or Comice. These breads bake in attractive fluted brioche molds or, if you prefer, in six-ounce custard cups or an ordinary muffin pan.

*This home-style meal of baked red and white kidney beans with slab bacon is accompanied by baked peppers and a fluted pear bread.*

### WHAT TO DRINK

This hearty, country-style menu calls for a fresh red wine to accompany it. A simple Chianti would be fine. A California Gamay would also be good.

## SHOPPING LIST AND STAPLES

1 pound smokehouse-style lean slab bacon
8 to 12 light green frying peppers
3 fresh plum tomatoes, or 1 pound canned
2 small ripe pears (about ¾ pound total weight)
1 orange
Medium-size onion
2 eggs
¼ cup milk
1 tablespoon unsalted butter
20-ounce can red kidney beans
20-ounce can white cannellini beans
¼ cup chicken stock, preferably homemade (see page 13),
   or canned (optional)
¼ cup olive oil (approximately)
Maple syrup (optional)
1 tablespoon Dijon mustard
Hot pepper sauce
1 cup all-purpose flour
½ cup whole wheat flour
⅔ cup granulated sugar
¼ cup brown sugar
1 teaspoon ground ginger
Salt and freshly ground black pepper

## UTENSILS

Food processor
Small saucepan
Roasting pan with rack
13-by-9-by-2-inch baking dish
Oval gratin dish
8 metal brioche molds, 8 six-ounce custard cups, or
   muffin pan
2 large bowls (or one, if using processor)
Flour sifter
Colander
Measuring cups and spoons
Chef's knife
Paring knife
Wooden spoon
Rubber spatula
Tongs
Pastry brush
Electric mixer

## START-TO-FINISH STEPS

1. Follow bacon and beans recipe steps 1 and 2.
2. Follow baked peppers recipe steps 1 through 4.

3. When bacon is removed and oven temperature is lowered, follow baked peppers recipe step 5.
4. While peppers are baking, follow pear breads recipe steps 1 and 2; then follow bacon and beans recipe steps 3 through 6.
5. Follow baked peppers recipe step 6 and bacon and beans recipe step 7.
6. While bacon and beans are baking, follow pear breads recipe steps 3 and 4.
7. Follow bacon and beans recipe step 8 and pear breads recipe step 5.
8. Follow pear breads recipe step 6.
9. Serve bacon and beans with baked peppers; pass sweet pear breads separately.

---

## RECIPES

### Slab Bacon Roasted on Red and White Beans

1 pound smokehouse-style lean slab bacon
20-ounce can red kidney beans
20-ounce can white cannellini beans
Medium-size onion
3 fresh plum tomatoes, or 1 pound canned
¼ cup brown sugar
1 teaspoon ground ginger
1 teaspoon salt
Generous grinding of black pepper
1 tablespoon Dijon mustard
4 dashes hot pepper sauce
¼ cup chicken stock, preferably homemade (approximately)

1. Preheat oven to 400 degrees.
2. Cut bacon into 4 chunks. Score fat deeply in a small diamond pattern, cutting down to lean streaks. Set bacon chunks on rack in roasting pan, scored side up, and roast 20 minutes. Remove bacon and reduce heat to 375 degrees.
3. In colander, drain and rinse both cans of beans.
4. In food processor or by hand, finely chop onion and tomatoes.
5. If using processor, add brown sugar, ginger, salt, pepper, mustard, and hot pepper sauce to tomato and onion mixture and process briefly. Otherwise, combine all ingredients in large bowl. Stir in beans.
6. Put mixture in shallow 13-by-9-inch baking dish and spread evenly with rubber spatula. Drizzle ¼ cup chicken stock or water over mixture. Liquid should not quite cover beans. Lay bacon chunks on top.
7. Bake 35 minutes. Check occasionally and add tablespoon or so of stock or water if beans seem to be drying out. When fully cooked, mixture should be moist, but not soupy.
8. Remove from oven and keep warm.

### Baked Green Peppers

8 to 12 light green frying peppers
¼ cup olive oil (approximately)

Salt
Freshly ground black pepper

1. Turn oven to 375 degrees.
2. Carefully wash and dry peppers.
3. Lightly brush bottom and sides of oval gratin dish with olive oil.
4. Brush peppers with remaining oil and arrange them in gratin dish. Sprinkle lightly with salt and pepper.
5. Bake peppers 15 to 20 minutes, turning once with tongs if they darken too much. They are done when they soften and wrinkle. They may also blacken—charring will intensify their flavor.
6. Remove peppers from oven and let cool to room temperature before serving.

### Sweet Pear Breads

½ cup whole wheat flour
1 cup all-purpose flour
2 eggs
⅔ cup granulated sugar
2 small ripe pears (about ¾ pound total weight)
¼ cup milk
1 tablespoon grated orange rind
1 tablespoon unsalted butter
Maple syrup (optional)

1. Chill brioche molds, custard cups, or muffin pan in freezer. Sift whole wheat and all-purpose flours together onto sheet of wax paper. Set aside.
2. In large bowl, with mixer at high speed, beat eggs and sugar until mixture becomes pale and lemon colored, about 5 minutes.
3. Peel and core pears and cut into ¼-inch dice.
4. With mixer at low speed, beat in milk. Gradually stir in flours until batter becomes smooth and creamy. Add orange rind and diced pears, gently stirring just enough to distribute them thoroughly throughout batter.
5. Melt butter in small saucepan. Remove molds from freezer and brush them with butter. Fill with pear batter. Bake 30 minutes or until toothpick inserted in center comes out clean.
6. Turn out onto individual plates and serve warm with maple syrup, if desired.

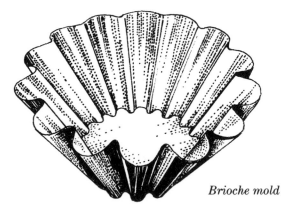

*Brioche mold*

# Smoked Sable and Salmon Rolls with Cream Cheese and Caviar
# Chicken Breasts Béarnaise / Leaf Lettuce and Mushroom Salad
# Broiled Peach Halves with Raspberry Jam

*Sable and salmon rolls, filled and decorated with two kinds of caviar, are appetizers for this brunch. The main course, a split*

*English muffin layered with chicken and sauce, is served with salad. Serve the broiled peaches separately.*

55

The first course in this menu calls for smoked sable and salmon, available at the delicatessen counters of most supermarkets. If the slices of smoked fish are too stiff to curve properly around the caviar filling, cut them into squares or triangles to make small sandwiches. Spread the cream cheese mixture to the edges; then dip the edges into the extra caviar to make an attractive rim. Smoked trout is a good substitute for sable. Golden whitefish caviar and red salmon caviar are sold in most supermarkets.

## WHAT TO DRINK

To make this elegant menu truly festive, choose a brut Champagne or a top-quality California sparkling white.

## SHOPPING LIST AND STAPLES

2 skinless, boneless chicken breasts (about 2 pounds total weight)
4 thin slices Smithfield ham or prosciutto
4 thin slices smoked salmon (about ¼ pound total weight)
4 thin slices smoked sable
2 ounces golden (whitefish) caviar
2 ounces red salmon caviar
Small head leaf lettuce
¼ pound mushrooms
4 large ripe peaches or nectarines
1 cucumber, preferably unwaxed (optional)
Small red bell pepper
2 large shallots
3 eggs
2 sticks unsalted butter
½ pint sour cream
3-ounce package cream cheese
6-ounce can jumbo-size pitted black olives
6 tablespoons olive oil
1½ tablespoons vegetable oil
¼ cup red wine vinegar
2 tablespoons tarragon vinegar
4 tablespoons raspberry jam
½ teaspoon Dijon mustard
4 English muffins
Small bunch fresh tarragon, or 1 teaspoon dried
Salt and freshly ground white pepper

## UTENSILS

Food processor or blender
Large skillet with cover
Medium-size saucepan
Small saucepan with cover
Small sauté pan
9-by-13-inch heatproof ceramic baking dish
Large bowl
4 small bowls
Strainer
Measuring spoons
Chef's knife
Paring knife
Slotted spoon
Teaspoon
Metal spatula
Rubber spatula
Whisk
Tongs
Salad spinner (optional)
Toaster

## START-TO-FINISH STEPS

**1.** Follow peach halves recipe steps 1 through 3.
**2.** For chicken béarnaise, separate eggs into 2 small bowls. Cover and refrigerate whites for other use. Mince shallots. Follow recipe steps 1 through 4.
**3.** Follow leaf lettuce salad recipe steps 1 through 4.
**4.** Follow sable and salmon rolls recipe steps 1 through 3.
**5.** Follow chicken béarnaise recipe steps 5 and 6.
**6.** Serve sable and salmon rolls.
**7.** Follow peach halves recipe step 4. While peaches are in broiler, follow chicken béarnaise recipe step 7.
**8.** Using tongs, remove peach halves to serving plate.
**9.** Follow chicken béarnaise recipe step 8.
**10.** Follow leaf lettuce salad recipe step 5.
**11.** Arrange chicken and salad together on plates, and serve with peaches.

## RECIPES

### Smoked Sable and Salmon Rolls with Cream Cheese and Caviar

3-ounce package cream cheese
2 tablespoons sour cream
4 thin slices smoked salmon (about ¼ pound)
2 ounces red salmon caviar

4 thin slices smoked sable
2 ounces golden (whitefish) caviar
Lettuce leaves for garnish (optional)
Cucumber slices for garnish (optional)

1. In small bowl, thoroughly blend cream cheese and sour cream.
2. Lay salmon slices on flat surface and, with rubber spatula, spread each with cheese mixture. Spoon red caviar down center of each and roll up slices. Repeat process with sable and golden caviar.
3. Arrange salmon and sable rolls on platter lined with lettuce and garnish with cucumber slices, if desired. Sprinkle remaining red and golden caviars over rolls. Cover loosely until ready to serve.

## Chicken Breasts Béarnaise

2 teaspoons minced shallots
1 tablespoon minced fresh tarragon, or 1 teaspoon crumbled dried
¼ cup red wine vinegar
2 skinless, boneless chicken breasts
4 thin slices Smithfield ham or prosciutto
3 egg yolks
½ teaspoon Dijon mustard
Freshly ground white pepper
2 sticks unsalted butter
1½ tablespoons vegetable oil
Salt
4 English muffins

1. In small sauté pan, combine shallots, tarragon, and vinegar and boil until liquid is reduced by half. Remove from heat to cool.
2. Halve chicken breasts; cut ham into julienne strips.
3. Put egg yolks into container of food processor or blender. Add mustard and a grinding of pepper. Strain reduced vinegar liquid into container and cover.
4. Clarify butter: In small saucepan, slowly heat 1 stick plus 4 tablespoons butter until melted and bubbling but not brown. Cover saucepan and remove from heat. Preheat oven to 200 degrees.
5. Heat large skillet and add oil and 2 tablespoons butter. Over medium heat, sauté chicken breasts about 2 minutes on each side, turning with metal spatula. Sprinkle with salt and pepper. Cook, covered, over low heat 15 minutes. Remove to heatproof platter and cover to keep warm.
6. Halve and toast English muffins. Butter muffins with

remaining butter and cover to keep warm.
7. Uncover melted butter. Milky residue at bottom is milk solids; clear golden liquid above is clarified butter. Carefully pour off clarified butter; discard solids. Start food processor or blender. After 5 seconds, remove cover and slowly drizzle in clarified butter, about ½ teaspoon at a time. Sauce should thicken to mayonnaise-like consistency.
8. Uncover English muffins and top with sautéed chicken breast halves and béarnaise sauce; garnish with julienned ham.

## Leaf Lettuce and Mushroom Salad

½ small head leaf lettuce
¼ pound medium-size mushrooms
½ small red bell pepper
4 jumbo-size black olives, pitted
2 tablespoons tarragon vinegar
Salt and freshly ground white pepper
6 tablespoons olive oil

1. Rinse lettuce and dry in salad spinner or pat dry with kitchen towel. Tear into bite-size pieces.
2. Clean mushrooms with damp paper towel and slice. Core, seed, and slice red pepper into strips. Slice black olives.
3. In large bowl, combine lettuce with mushrooms, red pepper, and olives. Refrigerate until ready to serve.
4. In small bowl, whisk together vinegar and salt and pepper to taste. Slowly drizzle in olive oil. Taste and adjust seasonings. Reserve.
5. Stir dressing to recombine. Pour dressing over salad and toss.

## Broiled Peach Halves with Raspberry Jam

4 large ripe peaches or nectarines
3 to 4 tablespoons raspberry jam

1. Bring 2 cups water to a boil in medium-size saucepan. Blanch peaches 30 seconds to loosen skins. Remove peaches with slotted spoon. Peel and halve them.
2. Butter heatproof ceramic baking dish.
3. Place peaches cut side up, removing thin slice from bottom of each half, if necessary, so they will stay upright. Set halves in dish and fill each cavity with raspberry jam.
4. Set dish under broiler about 3 inches from heat source. Broil 3 minutes, or until jam bubbles. Let rest a moment before serving.

# Bernice Hunt

MENU 1 (Left)
Champagne à l'Orange
Provençal Salad Platter
Cheese Pudding
Sliced Mangoes with Lime Wedges

MENU 2
Spinach Frittata
Tossed Green Salad
Apple Crisp

MENU 3
Artichokes with Lemon Butter
Saffron Rice with Sausages
Poached Apples in Orange Syrup

The author of some sixty books, Bernice Hunt describes herself as a dedicated "gourmet short-order cook" and prefers to spend her leisure hours with her guests rather than in the kitchen. Quick and elegant, the three brunches here contain no red meat or fancy desserts, which Bernice Hunt considers to be out of place at brunch. This is a meal that should satisfy but not overwhelm appetites and should induce conversation rather than the urge to take an afternoon nap.

All three menus feature combinations of fresh fruits and vegetables with sausages, cheese, or eggs. In Menu 1, a variation of the classic French Niçoise salad (named for the Mediterranean city of Nice and featuring black olives, anchovies, and tomatoes), precedes a cheese pudding and a dessert of sliced mangoes. The main dish in Menu 2 is a spinach frittata—an Italian-style omelet—which is served with a green salad and a sweet but not heavy apple crisp. Menu 3 offers saffron rice—the busy American cook's version of risotto—and sausages as the main course, with warm artichokes as an appetizer and orange-flavored apples for dessert.

*The red tomato slices, green lettuce, browned cheese pudding, and golden-yellow mango slices of this brunch would be colorful on any china, but dark plates make the foods look particularly dramatic. Champagne à l'Orange, a mixture of orange juice and champagne, will stay cool and effervescent if you chill the glasses briefly in the freezer before opening the champagne.*

59

# Spinach Frittata
# Tossed Green Salad
# Apple Crisp

*A spinach frittata, cut into wedges, and a light salad of chicory and lettuce constitute the main course here. If you wish, add warm French bread. Garnish the apple crisp with whipped cream and apple slices.*

To prepare the spinach for this classic frittata, remove the stems, then wash the leaves thoroughly in three changes of water to remove any grit. Shake off excess water and then steam the spinach. Cool it, squeeze out the excess water, and pat dry with paper towels.

## WHAT TO DRINK

Serve a light red wine—a young Chianti or Barbera from Italy or a California Pinot Noir.

## SHOPPING LIST AND STAPLES

1½ pounds fresh spinach
1 large onion
1 head Boston lettuce
Small head chicory
Small bunch parsley
Small bunch fresh basil, or ¼ teaspoon dried
1 clove garlic
6 tart crisp apples
1 lemon
2 sticks unsalted butter
5 eggs
2 tablespoons red wine vinegar
⅓ cup olive oil
1 cup brown sugar
¾ cup flour
½ teaspoon cinnamon
¼ teaspoon nutmeg
¼ teaspoon oregano
Salt and freshly ground pepper

## UTENSILS

Large skillet
Large saucepan
Deep pie plate or 2-quart baking dish
Large plate
Large bowl
Small bowl
Colander
Measuring cups and spoons
Chef's knife
Paring knife
Wooden spoon
Citrus grater
Wire whisk
Apple corer (optional)

## START-TO-FINISH STEPS

1. Follow apple crisp recipe steps 1 through 4.
2. Follow frittata recipe steps 1 through 4.
3. Follow salad recipe steps 1 and 2.
4. Follow frittata recipe step 5.
5. Follow salad recipe step 3 and frittata recipe step 6.
6. For dessert, serve apple crisp.

## RECIPES

### Spinach Frittata

4 tablespoons unsalted butter
1 large onion, chopped
1½ pounds fresh spinach
5 eggs
½ cup chopped parsley
¾ teaspoon chopped fresh basil, or ¼ teaspoon dried
¼ teaspoon oregano
Salt and freshly ground pepper

1. In large skillet, melt 2 tablespoons butter over medium heat. Add onion and sauté about 3 minutes.
2. Wash spinach well. Put it in large saucepan and cook over medium-low heat until spinach is wilted, about 3 to 4 minutes. Squeeze and pat dry; chop coarsely.
3. In large bowl, whisk eggs until fluffy. Stir in onion, spinach, parsley, basil, oregano, and salt and pepper.
4. Melt 1 tablespoon butter in skillet. Pour in eggs. Cook over low heat until nearly firm, 12 to 15 minutes.
5. Place large plate over skillet; invert frittata onto plate. Add remaining tablespoon butter to pan, then carefully slide frittata back into skillet and cook about 4 minutes. When bottom is golden, slide out onto large plate.
6. Cut frittata into wedges and serve.

### Tossed Green Salad

1 head Boston lettuce
Small head chicory
1 clove garlic, chopped
1 teaspoon salt
Freshly ground pepper
2 tablespoons red wine vinegar
⅓ cup olive oil

1. Wash greens; pat dry with paper towels. Tear into bite-size pieces. Place in salad bowl, cover, and refrigerate.
2. In small bowl, mash garlic and salt with fork. Add pepper and vinegar, and gradually whisk in oil.
3. Pour dressing over greens and toss.

### Apple Crisp

1 lemon
6 tart crisp apples, unpeeled, cored, and sliced
½ teaspoon cinnamon
¼ teaspoon nutmeg
1 cup brown sugar
¾ cup flour
1 stick unsalted butter, at room temperature

1. Preheat oven to 375 degrees.
2. Grate lemon rind; juice ½ lemon. Place apple slices in buttered deep pie plate. Sprinkle with lemon juice, lemon rind, spices, and ¼ cup sugar; toss well.
3. In small bowl, mix remaining sugar, flour, and butter until crumbly. Sprinkle over apples and pat down gently.
4. Bake about 30 to 40 minutes, until top is browned.

# Artichokes with Lemon Butter
# Saffron Rice with Sausages
# Poached Apples in Orange Syrup

*The rice and sausage main dish, fragrant with saffron, is attractive sprinkled with chopped parsley. Serve whole artichokes separately, as a first course; poached apples, flavored with orange zest, complete the meal.*

The main dish here calls for Italian Arborio rice, a short, plump grain that turns creamy-firm when cooked. It is available at Italian groceries, specialty food stores, and some supermarkets. You can use a medium-grain white rice instead, but do not use converted rice.

## WHAT TO DRINK

With this menu you could serve a fruity red wine, like Italian Dolcetto, French Beaujolais, or California Gamay.

## SHOPPING LIST AND STAPLES

4 Italian sweet sausages (about ¾ pound)
4 artichokes
Medium-size onion
4 large tart apples, preferably Granny Smith
1 medium-size juice orange
3 lemons
1 stick plus 5 tablespoons unsalted butter
¼ pound Parmesan cheese
13½-ounce can beef broth
1 cup rice, preferably Arborio
¼ teaspoon saffron threads
½ cup sugar
Salt and freshly ground pepper
2 tablespoons Marsala

## UTENSILS

Stockpot or kettle with cover
Small skillet
Large saucepan
Medium-size saucepan with cover
Small saucepan
Strainer
Measuring cups and spoons
Chef's knife
Paring knife
Wooden spoon
Slotted spoon
Grater

## START-TO-FINISH STEPS

1. Follow artichokes recipe steps 1 through 3.
2. While artichokes are cooking, follow rice recipe step 1.
3. Follow apples recipe steps 1 through 3.
4. Follow rice recipe steps 2 and 3.
5. While rice cooks, follow artichokes recipe step 4; serve.
6. Follow rice recipe step 4 and serve.
7. For dessert, follow apples recipe step 4.

## RECIPES

### Artichokes with Lemon Butter

2 lemons
4 artichokes
Salt
1 stick unsalted butter
Freshly ground pepper

1. Bring 3 to 4 quarts water to a boil in stockpot or kettle.
2. Cut 1 lemon into wedges. Wash and trim artichokes. Rub cut surfaces with lemon wedges as you work.
3. Put artichokes into stockpot and add salt. Cook, covered, 35 to 40 minutes, or until tender. Remove with slotted spoon and drain upside down on paper towels.
4. Juice remaining lemon; strain juice. In small saucepan, melt butter. Stir in lemon juice, salt, and pepper. Turn artichokes right side up; serve with lemon butter.

### Saffron Rice with Sausages

4 Italian sweet sausages (about ¾ pound)
5 tablespoons unsalted butter
Medium-size onion, chopped
1 cup rice, preferably Arborio
2 tablespoons Marsala
¼ teaspoon saffron threads, crushed
13½-ounce can beef broth, plus ½ can water
½ cup freshly grated Parmesan cheese
Salt

1. Prick sausages with fork and cook in small skillet until brown and thoroughly done, about 8 to 12 minutes. Drain on paper towels, then slice and return to pan.
2. In medium-size saucepan, melt 2 tablespoons butter. Add onion and sauté over medium heat until translucent. Add rice and stir until faintly golden, about 5 minutes.
3. Add Marsala, saffron, broth, and water. Bring to a boil, stir, reduce heat to low, and cover pan. Cook about 20 minutes, stirring several times.
4. Five minutes before rice is done, quickly reheat sausage slices. Add remaining 3 tablespoons butter, grated cheese, and sliced sausages to rice mixture; stir gently to combine. Transfer to serving dish.

### Poached Apples in Orange Syrup

½ cup sugar
4 large tart apples, preferably Granny Smith, cored
1 tablespoon grated orange rind
⅓ cup orange juice
2 tablespoons lemon juice

1. In large saucepan, bring sugar and ½ cup water to a boil. Cook, uncovered and without stirring, over medium heat 5 minutes, or until reduced by half.
2. Peel apples about one third of the way down.
3. Using slotted spoon, add apples to syrup, turning them until coated on all sides. Set right side up and cover pan. Reduce heat and simmer gently until apples are just soft, about 10 to 12 minutes; transfer to serving dish.
4. Add grated rind and orange and lemon juices to syrup and cook over high heat until thick, about 3 to 5 minutes. Pour syrup over apples and serve.

# Christopher Styler

As a professional recipe developer and chef, Christopher Styler works long hours in elaborate kitchens. So, when he entertains at Sunday brunch, he wants to avoid time-consuming procedures. "Food for entertaining does not have to be a three-day affair," he says, "but cooks should spend time choosing quality ingredients and preparing them well." He serves homey food and, for the convenience of his guests, buys two copies of the Sunday paper.

Another of Christopher Styler's brunch strategies is to completely eliminate last-minute fuss by assembling all the meal's components beforehand. The smorgasbord of Menu 1 is a perfect example of a pre-assembled meal. The Swedish *smörgasbord*—literally, "sandwich tables"—is a carefully prepared and arranged banquet that customarily features a range of cold, room temperature, and piping hot dishes, possibly as many as 60 at a time. This abbreviated version keeps to that format.

Rather than requiring complete pre-assembling, Menus 2 and 3 are so simple that they call for minimal last-minute preparation. In Menu 2, you can ready the fruit for the salad ahead of time and, in Menu 3, prepare the Cranberry Fool first thing in the morning.

*This small-scale smorgasbord consists of two fish plates: sliced smoked sable, with ramekins of radish and carrot salad, and freshly prepared herring in a sour cream and scallion dressing. The browned potato cake is served in wedges. Serve the grapes, strawberries, and cubed pineapple in individual bowls.*

# Salt Herring with Sour Cream and Scallions
# Smoked Sable Platter
# Oven-Baked Potato Cake/Sesame Fruit Salad

According to Swedish tradition, herring is always eaten first at a smorgasbord. Christopher Styler prepares his version from scratch and calls for salt herring. Salt herring often is available at delicatessens or at the delicatessen sections of supermarkets.

Smoked sable is the main ingredient of the second fish platter. Oilier and richer than smoked salmon, sable is available at some delicatessens.

In addition to Norwegian flatbread, bagels are a welcome component of this buffet. Toast them in the oven before serving.

## WHAT TO DRINK

The herring and the sable here need white wines; try a Gewürztraminer from Alsace or one from California.

## SHOPPING LIST AND STAPLES

1 pound salt herring fillets
¾ pound thinly sliced smoked sable
3 large baking potatoes (about 1¾ pounds total weight)
Large carrot
1 bunch or bag radishes (about 8 ounces, trimmed)
Small head leaf lettuce, preferably Romaine (optional)
Small bunch parsley
Small bunch scallions
Small pineapple
1 orange
1 lemon
1 bunch green grapes (about ½ pound total weight)
1 pint strawberries or ½ pint raspberries
2 sticks unsalted butter (approximately)
½ cup sour cream
Bagels and pumpernickel bread
Norwegian flatbread (optional)
2 tablespoons honey
1 ounce sesame seeds
¼ teaspoon sugar
Salt
Freshly ground pepper

## UTENSILS

Food processor (if not using grater)
Medium-size skillet
Small saucepan
9-inch nonstick round cake pan
3 large bowls
Medium-size bowl
2 small bowls
Colander
Coarse-mesh sieve
Measuring cups and spoons
Chef's knife
Paring knife
Wooden spoons
Grater
Vegetable peeler
Citrus juicer (optional)
Pastry brush

## START-TO-FINISH STEPS

*The night before:* Follow herring recipe step 1.

**1.** Follow potato cake recipe steps 1 through 6.
**2.** While potato cake is baking, chop parsley and follow smoked sable recipe steps 1 through 3.
**3.** Grate rind and squeeze juice from lemon. Follow herring recipe steps 1 through 4.
**4.** Follow fruit salad recipe steps 1 through 5.
**5.** Just before potato cake is done, follow herring recipe step 5 and smoked sable recipe step 4. Then follow potato cake recipe step 7 and serve with herring and sable.
**6.** For dessert, follow fruit salad recipe step 6.

## RECIPES

## Salt Herring with Sour Cream and Scallions

1 pound salt herring fillets
3 scallions
½ cup sour cream
1 teaspoon lemon juice
½ teaspoon grated lemon rind
½ teaspoon freshly ground pepper
Bagels and pumpernickel bread
Norwegian flatbread (optional)

**1.** Place herring fillets in large bowl of cold water to cover. Refrigerate overnight, changing water once.
**2.** Pour off water and drain herring fillets on paper towels.
**3.** Trim scallions, leaving green tops. With flat side of chef's knife, bruise scallions and cut crosswise into thin slices. Cut herring into bite-size pieces.

**4.** In small bowl, stir together sour cream, lemon juice and rind, pepper, and scallions. Add herring and stir until well coated. Let stand at room temperature until ready to serve.

**5.** Serve herring in bowl or mound it in center of small serving platter. Accompany with a selection of bagels, pumpernickel slices, and Norwegian flatbread, if desired.

## Smoked Sable Platter

1 bunch or bag radishes (about 8 ounces, trimmed)
Large carrot
2 tablespoons chopped parsley
1 tablespoon lemon juice
¼ teaspoon sugar
Salt
Freshly ground pepper
Lettuce leaves for garnish, preferably Romaine (optional)
¾ pound thinly sliced smoked sable

**1.** Trim radishes. Wash under cold running water and pat dry with paper towels. Using small holes of grater, grate radishes into medium-size bowl or grate them in food processor fitted with shredding disk. You should have about 1½ cups.

**2.** Peel and trim carrot. Grate as you did the radishes.

**3.** Place shredded vegetables in coarse-mesh sieve and, using back of spoon, press to extract juices. Transfer vegetables to medium-size bowl. Add parsley, lemon juice, sugar, and salt and pepper to taste; toss. Cover and refrigerate.

**4.** When ready to serve, toss once more. Divide salad among individual bowls and place them in center of serving platter lined with lettuce leaves, if desired. Arrange sable slices next to bowls.

## Oven-Baked Potato Cake

4 tablespoons unsalted butter
3 large baking potatoes (about 1¾ pounds total weight)
1 teaspoon salt
¼ teaspoon freshly ground pepper

**1.** Preheat oven to 450 degrees. In small saucepan, melt butter. Remove from heat.

**2.** Lightly brush 9-inch nonstick round cake pan with enough melted butter to grease pan well; set pan aside.

**3.** Pour 2 cups cold water into large bowl. Working quickly, peel 1 potato and grate it directly into water. After all potatoes are peeled and grated, line colander with clean kitchen towel or cheesecloth and pour contents of bowl into colander. Gather towel or cheesecloth around potatoes and squeeze to remove excess water.

**4.** Place cake pan in oven to heat while you finish preparing potatoes.

**5.** Dry bowl and add remaining melted butter, salt, and pepper. Add potatoes and toss until evenly coated.

**6.** Remove pan from oven and add potatoes, pressing lightly to form even layer. Bake until cake is tender in the center and golden brown outside, about 40 minutes.

**7.** Place large plate over cake and, holding pan and plate together with 2 pot holders, invert cake quickly onto plate. Cover inverted cake with 12-inch serving platter and again quickly invert, top side up. Cut into wedges and serve at once.

## Sesame Fruit Salad

2 tablespoons sesame seeds
2 tablespoons honey
2 teaspoons orange juice
Small pineapple
1 pint strawberries or ½ pint raspberries
½ pound seedless green grapes

**1.** In medium-size ungreased skillet, toast sesame seeds over medium-high heat, shaking skillet frequently to keep seeds from scorching. When they smell toasty, remove from heat and let cool.

**2.** In small bowl, stir honey and orange juice until combined. Stir in sesame seeds.

**3.** With chef's knife, trim off leafy top of pineapple. Cut into quarters lengthwise. Then, with paring knife, trim hard center core from each quarter. Cut flesh from outside rind and trim off any "eyes." Cut into 1-inch cubes.

**4.** In colander, rinse strawberries or raspberries briefly under cool water. Drain and gently pat dry with paper towels. If using strawberries, hull berries and halve, if desired. Rinse and dry grapes.

**5.** Put all fruit in large bowl and toss gently with honey dressing. Refrigerate, covered.

**6.** Just before serving, toss gently once more.

---

ADDED TOUCH

If you have the time, you can add this simple salad to your smorgasbord-type meal.

## Shredded Lettuce Vinaigrette

1 head leaf lettuce, preferably Romaine
1 small red bell pepper
1½ tablespoons red wine vinegar
½ teaspoon Dijon mustard
Salt
Freshly ground pepper
¼ cup peanut oil

**1.** Remove any wilted or bruised outer lettuce leaves; core lettuce. Separate into individual leaves and rinse thoroughly under cool running water. Dry in salad spinner or pat dry with paper towels. Cut leaves crosswise into thin shreds. Place in salad bowl.

**2.** Core and seed pepper; cut lengthwise into thin strips. Add to salad bowl and toss. Cover and refrigerate.

**3.** In small bowl, combine vinegar, mustard, and salt and pepper to taste. Beating vigorously with fork, add oil in a slow, steady stream. Set aside.

**4.** Just before serving, beat dressing to recombine. Pour over vegetables and toss to coat.

# Corned-Beef Hash with Sour Cream and Mustard Sauce
# Watercress and Orange Salad
# Strawberries and Honeydew in Champagne

*Chunky corned-beef hash is served with a watercress and orange salad and fruit tossed with Champagne dressing.*

Hash is a mixture of cooked foods minced separately, then combined for recooking by baking or frying. It can include almost anything. This basic hash calls for a few simple ingredients; it should be creamy, just wet enough to hold together, and unmold in one piece. Use a well-seasoned cast-iron or nonstick skillet.

## WHAT TO DRINK

Hash is a robust dish; serve anything from the same sparkling wine you use in the fruit recipe to a fruity red wine like a California Gamay or an Italian Dolcetto.

## SHOPPING LIST AND STAPLES

1½ pounds cooked corned beef, trimmed
3 medium-size boiling potatoes
5 to 6 small fresh mushrooms
1 bunch celery
Large onion
Large bunch watercress
Small honeydew melon
1 pint strawberries
1 navel orange
1 lemon

70

1 lime
Small piece fresh ginger
2 tablespoons unsalted butter
1 cup sour cream
5 tablespoons peanut oil
1 tablespoon white wine vinegar
2 tablespoons Dijon mustard
1 tablespoon sugar
Salt and freshly ground pepper
1 split (250 ml) dry Champagne or sparkling white wine

## UTENSILS

Large heavy-gauge skillet
Large saucepan
Salad bowl
Large bowl
2 medium-size bowls
2 small bowls
Colander
Measuring cups and spoons
Chef's knife
Paring knife
Wooden spoon
Metal spatula
Wire whisk
Vegetable peeler
Salad spinner (optional)

## START-TO-FINISH STEPS

1. Follow salad recipe steps 1 through 4.
2. Wash, dry, and chop celery leaves. Peel and dice onion. Follow hash recipe steps 1 through 5.
3. As hash is cooking and browning, peel and mince ginger and follow strawberries recipe steps 1 through 3.
4. Prepare sour cream and mustard sauce. Follow salad recipe step 5 and hash recipe step 6.
5. For dessert, follow strawberries recipe step 4.

## RECIPES

### Corned-Beef Hash with Sour Cream and Mustard Sauce

1½ pounds cooked corned beef, trimmed
3 medium size boiling potatoes
2 tablespoons unsalted butter
Large onion, peeled and diced
5 to 6 small fresh mushrooms sliced
2 tablespoons peanut oil
Salt and freshly ground pepper
½ cup coarsely chopped celery leaves
Sour cream and mustard sauce (see following recipe)

1. With chef's knife, cut corned beef into ½-inch pieces.
2. Peel potatoes and cut into ½-inch cubes. Place in large saucepan with cold water to cover. Bring to a boil and simmer 5 minutes.

3. Drain potatoes in colander; pat dry with paper towels. In large heavy-gauge skillet, heat oil and butter until butter foams. Add onion and mushrooms to skillet, and sauté, stirring, until onion is soft about 3 minutes.
4. Add potatoes to skillet. Season to taste with salt and pepper. Continue sautéing until potatoes begin to soften around the edges, about 5 minutes.
5. Add corned beef and celery leaves. Continue cooking, using metal spatula to scrape browned bottom crust into hash. After about 10 minutes, stop scraping and allow crust to form. Cook until potatoes are tender and hash is browned, about another 5 minutes. Add a few tablespoons water if mixture begins to stick.
6. Serve hash from skillet, with sauce on the side.

### Sour Cream and Mustard Sauce

In small bowl, combine 1 cup sour cream, 2 tablespoons Dijon mustard, and 2 tablespoons lemon juice.

### Watercress and Orange Salad

1 navel orange
1 tablespoon white wine vinegar
3 tablespoons peanut oil
Salt and freshly ground pepper
Large bunch watercress

1. Using paring knife, remove peel and pith from orange, working over small bowl to catch juice. Remove membranes and set orange sections aside.
2. Measure 2 tablespoons juice into bowl and add vinegar. Whisk in oil and salt and pepper to taste.
3. Cut any thick orange sections in half lengthwise; add sections to dressing. Macerate at room temperature.
4. Trim watercress and rinse. Dry in salad spinner or pat dry with paper towels. Place in large salad bowl and refrigerate.
5. To serve, toss watercress with oranges and dressing.

### Strawberries and Honeydew in Champagne

Small honeydew melon
1 pint strawberries
1 tablespoon sugar
1 tablespoon lime juice
1 teaspoon minced fresh ginger
1 split (250 ml) dry champagne or sparkling white wine

1. With chef's knife, halve honeydew; scoop out seeds. Cut into quarters and cut flesh away from rind. Cut flesh into bite-size chunks. Place in large bowl, cover, and refrigerate until ready to serve.
2. Rinse strawberries briefly in cool water. Gently pat dry with paper towels. Hull berries. Leave whole or cut in half. Place in medium-size bowl, cover, and refrigerate.
3. In medium-size bowl, combine sugar, lime juice, and ginger. Set aside.
4. Just before serving, stir champagne into ginger mixture. Pour dressing over both bowls of fruit and toss. In serving bowl, arrange honeydew around strawberries.

# Warm Salad of Turkey and Vegetables
# Cranberry Fool

*The main-course turkey and vegetable salad and the cranberry dessert would be an appetizing post-Thanksgiving meal.*

For this unusual warm salad entrée, you can easily slice the fennel into julienne: cut off the stalks and trim away the roots, slice through the fennel bulb crosswise at half-inch intervals, then quarter these rounds, forming the julienne. If you substitute green beans for snow peas, blanch them first. Crusty French bread with a garlic-flavored butter should accompany the salad.

## WHAT TO DRINK
Choose either a full-bodied white wine, such as a Chardonnay, or a soft red wine, such as a Pinot Noir.

## SHOPPING LIST AND STAPLES
¾ pound cooked turkey
Small head red cabbage
¼ pound snow peas or green beans
1 fennel bulb
Small red onion
Small red bell pepper
1 head chicory
1 juice orange
12-ounce package fresh cranberries
1½ cups heavy cream

2 tablespoons chicken stock, preferably homemade
   (see page 13), or canned
⅓ cup peanut oil
¼ cup white wine vinegar
½ cup granulated sugar
2 tablespoons confectioners' sugar
¾ teaspoon salt
¼ teaspoon freshly ground pepper

## UTENSILS

Large heavy-gauge skillet with cover
Nonaluminum saucepan
2 large bowls
Small bowl
Colander
Food mill or coarse sieve
Measuring spoons and cups
Chef's knife
Paring knife
2 wooden spoons
Slotted spoon
Rubber spatula
Citrus juicer
Salad spinner (optional)
Electric mixer

## START-TO-FINISH STEPS

**1.** Juice orange and follow cranberry recipe step 1.
**2.** While cranberries macerate, follow turkey salad recipe step 1.
**3.** Chill bowl and beaters for whipped cream and follow cranberry recipe steps 2 and 3.
**4.** While cranberries cool, follow turkey salad recipe steps 2 through 5.
**5.** While salad marinates, follow cranberry recipe steps 4 and 5.
**6.** Follow turkey salad recipe steps 6 and 7.
**7.** Serve cranberry fool for dessert.

## RECIPES

### Warm Salad of Turkey and Vegetables

¼ pound snow peas or green beans
1 fennel bulb
Small red bell pepper
¼ head small red cabbage
Small red onion
¾ pound cooked turkey
⅓ cup peanut oil
¼ cup white wine vinegar
2 tablespoons chicken stock
¾ teaspoon salt
¼ teaspoon freshly ground pepper
Chicory leaves

**1.** In colander, rinse snow peas, fennel, red pepper, and cabbage; drain. Dry in salad spinner or pat dry with paper towels. Prepare as follows: Remove strings from snow peas. Trim feathery greens from fennel bulb; quarter and slice into julienne strips, taking care to trim around core. Cut red pepper in half and remove stem, ribs, and seeds; slice into ¼-inch strips. Shred cabbage with grater or in food processor fitted with shredding disk. Peel onion and cut in half; then cut each half into ½-inch slices. Cover vegetables.
**2.** Cut turkey into julienne strips.
**3.** In large heavy-gauge skillet, heat 2 tablespoons oil over medium-high heat. Add onion, fennel, and cabbage. Sauté, stirring frequently with wooden spoon, until softened and lightly browned, about 5 minutes. Add red pepper and turkey; stir until heated, about 4 minutes.
**4.** Reduce heat to medium-low. Add snow peas, vinegar, stock, salt, and pepper. Cover and cook, shaking pan, until peas turn bright green, about 3 minutes.
**5.** Using slotted spoon, transfer vegetables and turkey to large bowl. Add remaining oil to skillet. Simmer, scraping sides and bottom of pan to remove any brown bits, until liquid is reduced to ⅓ cup, about 3 minutes. Pour dressing over vegetable and turkey mixture. Let stand about 15 minutes, tossing occasionally.
**6.** Rinse chicory with cold water to remove all grit. Trim away any wilted or brown spots. Dry in salad spinner or pat dry with paper towels.
**7.** Line individual plates with chicory leaves. Top with salad. Drizzle any dressing left in bowl over salad.

### Cranberry Fool

12-ounce package fresh cranberries
½ cup granulated sugar
3 tablespoons fresh orange juice
1½ cups heavy cream, chilled
2 tablespoons confectioners' sugar

**1.** In colander, rinse cranberries briefly under cool water and drain. Pick out stems and any damaged berries. Transfer to medium-size nonaluminum saucepan. Stir in granulated sugar and orange juice. Stir to mix and macerate 10 minutes, tossing occasionally.
**2.** Cook cranberries over medium heat, stirring occasionally with wooden spoon, until liquid comes to a boil, about 5 minutes. Increase heat to medium-high and boil, covered, until cranberries have burst and mixture is fairly thick, about another 5 minutes. Stir occasionally.
**3.** Remove from heat. Let cool, stirring occasionally, until lukewarm, about 15 minutes.
**4.** Put through food mill or force through coarse sieve into small bowl. There should be about 1 cup purée.
**5.** Using electric mixer, whip cream in large chilled bowl until soft peaks form. Continue beating, gradually adding confectioners' sugar, until cream forms stiff peaks. With rubber spatula, partially fold in cranberry mixture, leaving thin streaks. Spoon into individual glasses. Refrigerate, covered, until ready to serve.

# Henry Lewis Creel

**MENU 1 (Left)**
Individual Meat Loaves with Mushroom Sauce
Wilted Lettuce Salad
Old-Fashioned Bread Pudding

**MENU 2**
Chili Soup with Polenta and Chopped Vegetables
Bananas Flambée

**MENU 3**
Fish Soup
Corn Muffins
Spiced Pear Crisp

E conomy—of time, motion, ingredients, calories, and cost—defines the cooking style of Henry Lewis Creel, a New York-based cookbook author and retired businessman. Twenty years ago, because he was overweight, this self-taught cook developed his own version of "lean cooking": he scaled down his personal recipes to provide modest single portions that satisfied but did not offer him the chance to overeat. In the process, he lost weight as well. Now, he does not eliminate calorie-laden foods altogether from his diet, but his total daily food intake is moderate.

His recipes-for-one are building blocks for his three brunch menus. By increasing proportions of certain ingredients, he has devised uncomplicated meals that will leave you without leftovers. He emphasizes simplicity—too many ingredients spoil the recipe, he believes. Menus 1 and 3 are home-style meals that would suit family occasions. Menu 2, a celebratory brunch, features a Tex-Mex chili soup with Italian polenta, followed by rum-flavored flamed bananas for dessert.

*You can arrange the individual meat loaves with the mushroom sauce on a large serving platter garnished with tomato slices and escarole. Serve the wilted lettuce salad with the meal. The browned bread pudding, garnished with cinnamon sticks, comes to the table in its baking dish.*

75

# Individual Meat Loaves with Mushroom Sauce
# Wilted Lettuce Salad
# Old-Fashioned Bread Pudding

The meat loaves for this brunch call for round steak, a relatively lean cut of beef. Ask your butcher to trim away excess fat and to grind the meat. When you shop for ingredients for the sauce, select mushrooms with tightly closed caps that fit snugly over the stems and cover the gills on the underside. Small mushrooms, the least expensive, are ideal for chopping and slicing. Stored unwashed in a loosely covered container in the refrigerator, they will last from three to five days. When you are ready to use them, wipe them with a damp paper towel to remove any grit. Never soak mushrooms, because they will absorb water and lose their flavor.

Bread pudding, a rich dessert that probably originated in England, concludes this simple meal. Use a 3-cup ovenproof glass or stoneware baking dish or standard-size muffin cups.

## WHAT TO DRINK

The direct, basic flavors of this menu need equally uncomplicated beverages. The cook suggests cold beer. You could also serve a red wine—perhaps an inexpensive Merlot from California or Italy.

## SHOPPING LIST AND STAPLES

1 pound ground round steak
2 slices bacon
2 medium-size onions
1 medium-size carrot
¼ pound mushrooms
1 head Boston or other leaf lettuce
1 stalk celery
2 eggs
3 cups milk
2 tablespoons plus 2 teaspoons unsalted butter
2 tablespoons red wine vinegar
3 slices white bread
3 tablespoons golden raisins
2 tablespoons flour
2 tablespoons plus 2 teaspoons sugar
¼ teaspoon ground cinnamon
Cinnamon sticks (optional)
¼ teaspoon nutmeg
Salt
Freshly ground pepper
1 teaspoon white peppercorns

## UTENSILS

Food processor or blender
Small sauté pan or skillet
Medium-size saucepan
Baking dish or baking sheet
3-cup baking dish or muffin pan
Salad bowl
Small bowl
Large mixing bowl (if not using food processor)
Measuring cups and spoons
Chef's knife
Paring knife
Wooden spoon
Rubber spatula
Slotted spatula
Whisk
Grater
Vegetable peeler
Rolling pin
Salad spinner (optional)

## START-TO-FINISH STEPS

1. Follow salad recipe step 1.
2. Follow meat loaves recipe steps 1 through 5.
3. For mushroom sauce, grate onion and clean mushrooms with damp paper towels. Dice mushrooms.
4. Follow bread pudding recipe steps 1 through 3.
5. When meat loaves have been in the oven 20 minutes, follow bread pudding recipe step 4.
6. Follow mushroom sauce recipe steps 1 through 3 and salad recipe steps 2 and 3.
7. Remove meat loaves from oven, step 6, follow salad recipe step 4, and serve meat loaves with mushroom sauce, step 7.
8. Remove bread pudding from oven, step 5, and serve for dessert.

## RECIPES

### Individual Meat Loaves with Mushroom Sauce

1 teaspoon white peppercorns
1 medium-size onion
1 medium-size carrot
1 stalk celery

1 slice white bread
1 pound ground round steak
1 egg
Salt
Mushroom sauce (see following recipe)

1. Preheat oven to 350 degrees.
2. Put peppercorns between 2 sheets of wax paper and crush with rolling pin. Peel and coarsely slice onion. Wash, peel, and cut carrot into 1-inch slices. Wash, trim, and cut celery into 1-inch slices.
3. In food processor fitted with metal blade or in blender, process vegetables a few seconds at a time, stopping occasionally to scrape down sides of bowl with rubber spatula, until mixture is completely combined. Or use chef's knife to chop onion, carrot, and celery. Crumble bread into large mixing bowl. Add chopped vegetables, peppercorns, meat, egg, and salt to taste; use your hands to mix well.
4. Divide mixture into 4 portions and, with damp hands, mold each into a round loaf. Place meat loaves in baking dish or on baking sheet lined with aluminum foil, with sides folded up all around to hold in meat juices.
5. Bake meat loaves 30 minutes.
6. When done, remove from oven and cool slightly.
7. Serve with mushroom sauce.

## Mushroom Sauce

2 tablespoons unsalted butter
1 tablespoon grated onion
1 cup diced mushrooms (about ¼ pound)
2 tablespoons flour
1 cup milk
Salt
Freshly ground pepper

1. Melt butter in saucepan and cook onion 1 minute, stirring constantly with wooden spoon.
2. Add diced mushrooms. Stir, and continue cooking over low heat 1 minute.
3. Sprinkle mixture with flour. Stir well to combine, and cook 1 to 2 minutes. Then pour in milk. Continue to cook, still stirring, until sauce thickens. Add salt and pepper to taste. Cover and keep warm until serving time.

## Wilted Lettuce Salad

1 head Boston or other leaf lettuce
2 slices bacon

2 tablespoons red wine vinegar
2 tablespoons water
2 teaspoons sugar

1. Wash lettuce and dry in salad spinner or pat dry with paper towels. Tear into bite-size pieces, discarding core and any blemished leaves; put in salad bowl. Refrigerate until ready to use.
2. In skillet used for bread pudding, fry bacon until crisp.
3. Using slotted spatula, remove bacon from pan and drain on plate lined with paper towels. Pour off all but 2 teaspoons of bacon drippings. Add vinegar, water, and sugar. Cook over medium heat, stirring, 1 minute.
4. Crumble bacon over lettuce. Pour hot vinegar dressing over salad and toss well. Serve at once.

## Old-Fashioned Bread Pudding

2 slices white bread
2 cups milk
2 teaspoons butter
1 egg
2 tablespoons sugar
¼ teaspoon cinnamon
¼ teaspoon nutmeg
3 tablespoons golden raisins
Cinnamon sticks for garnish (optional)

1. To make bread crumbs, process bread in food processor fitted with metal blade or in blender. Pour milk into medium-size bowl, add bread crumbs, and soak 1 minute.
2. Melt butter in skillet. Butter 3-cup baking dish or 4 muffin cups with melted butter.
3. Using whisk, beat egg in small bowl; add egg, sugar, spices, and raisins to bread crumbs and milk mixture. Using wooden spoon, stir several minutes to ensure that sugar and egg are completely blended.
4. Pour batter into baking dish or divide among muffin cups. Bake 35 to 40 minutes.
5. Serve hot. Garnish with cinnamon sticks, if desired.

---

ADDED TOUCH

A platter of cut-up fresh fruit would be a good beginning for this meal. Serve pineapple chunks, orange segments, unpared apple wedges (sprinkled with lemon juice to prevent discoloration), and whole strawberries; garnish the platter with mint sprigs.

# Chili Soup with Polenta and Chopped Vegetables
# Bananas Flambée

*Chili soup and polenta, topped with chopped onion, green pepper, celery, tomato, and lettuce, is excellent for a winter Sunday. If you wish, offer crusty brown bread. The flamed bananas, split lengthwise, are garnished with orange zest.*

H enry Lewis Creel likes to combine the spicy taste of a southwestern chili soup with the blandness of polenta, an Italian cornmeal dish that ordinarily requires a lengthy cooking time. Here, unlike the slow, cook-and-stir Italian method, you blend the cornmeal with water and, over medium heat, stir only until the mixture starts to thicken. It will finish cooking in 10 minutes.

## WHAT TO DRINK

The chili precludes any delicate wines with this menu; serve cold, dark Mexican beer or ale.

## SHOPPING LIST AND STAPLES

1 pound ground round steak
2 medium-size plus 1 small onion
2 cloves garlic
1 head Romaine lettuce
1 small green pepper
1 small tomato
1 stalk celery
1 large orange
4 medium-size firm bananas
1 tablespoon unsalted butter
16-ounce can peeled Italian plum tomatoes
2 sixteen-ounce cans kidney beans
¼ cup honey
3 tablespoons vegetable oil
¼ cup yellow cornmeal
Salt
½ teaspoon crushed red pepper
2 tablespoons chili powder
1 teaspoon ground cumin
1 teaspoon oregano
¼ teaspoon nutmeg
¾ teaspoon cinnamon
¼ cup sherry
2 tablespoons light rum

## UTENSILS

Large heavy-gauge saucepan with cover
Medium-size heavy-gauge saucepan with cover
Small saucepan
13-by-9-by-2-inch baking dish
Small bowl
Measuring spoons and cups

Chef's knife
Paring knife
Wooden spoons
Juicer
Lemon zester
Flame tamer or asbestos mat

## START-TO-FINISH STEPS

1. Follow chili soup recipe steps 1 through 4.
2. While chili soup is cooking, prepare vegetable garnishes.
3. About 20 minutes before chili soup is done, follow bananas recipe steps 1 through 5.
4. Follow chili soup recipe steps 5 through 7.
5. Twenty minutes before dessert is to be served, follow step 6 of bananas recipe.
6. Follow bananas recipe steps 7 and 8, and serve.

## RECIPES

### Chili Soup with Polenta and Chopped Vegetables

2 medium-size onions
2 cloves garlic
2 to 3 tablespoons vegetable oil
1 to 2 tablespoons chili powder
1 pound ground round steak
Salt
½ teaspoon crushed red pepper
1 teaspoon ground cumin
1 teaspoon oregano
16-ounce can peeled Italian plum tomatoes, plus an equal volume of water
2 sixteen-ounce cans kidney beans, undrained
¼ cup yellow cornmeal
1 cup water
2 cups coarsely chopped Romaine lettuce for garnish
¼ cup chopped onion for garnish
¼ cup chopped green bell pepper for garnish
¼ cup chopped celery for garnish
¼ cup peeled, seeded, and chopped tomato for garnish

1. Chop onions and mince garlic. Heat oil in large saucepan and, stirring constantly with wooden spoon, sauté onions, garlic, and chili powder 1 minute.
2. Add ground round steak. Stir to break meat into small pieces and cook 3 to 4 minutes or until meat loses its red color.
3. Add salt to taste, seasonings, tomatoes, and water, and stir to combine with meat and onions. Then gently stir in beans and their liquid.
4. Bring to simmer, partially cover, and cook over low heat 40 minutes, stirring occasionally.
5. In medium-size saucepan with tight-fitting cover, combine cornmeal and water. Stirring with wooden spoon, cook uncovered, over medium heat, until mixture just begins to thicken, about 3 minutes.
6. Cover tightly and reduce heat to very low, using flame tamer or asbestos mat. Stir occasionally and cook until polenta is thick and holds its shape, about 10 minutes.
7. To serve, spoon soup into 4 individual soup bowls. Garnish each with a spoonful of polenta, chopped lettuce, onion, green pepper, celery, and tomato.

### Bananas Flambée

1 large orange
4 medium-size firm bananas
1 tablespoon unsalted butter
¼ cup honey
¼ cup sherry
½ to ¾ teaspoon cinnamon
¼ teaspoon nutmeg
2 tablespoons light rum

1. Preheat oven to 350 degrees.
2. Peel zest from orange, cut into julienne strips, and reserve. You should have about 3 tablespoons. Juice orange and measure ¼ cup juice.
3. Peel bananas and split lengthwise. Halve crosswise, on the diagonal.
4. Melt butter in small saucepan. Pour butter into large baking or gratin dish. Rotate dish to cover it with melted butter. Add bananas. Sprinkle with orange zest strips.
5. Using wooden spoon, in small bowl mix honey, orange juice, sherry, and spices thoroughly. Pour over bananas.
6. Place baking dish in oven and bake 20 minutes.
7. Remove bananas from oven and pour rum over them. Avert your face and carefully ignite rum. When flame dies, remove bananas to 4 serving plates.
8. Transfer remaining honey mixture from baking dish to saucepan in which butter was melted and boil sauce down, a minute or so, until it thickens and becomes syrupy. Pour syrup over bananas and serve hot.

# Fish Soup
# Corn Muffins
# Spiced Pear Crisp

*Serve the chunky fish soup with corn muffins and butter on the side, and garnish the pear crisp with lemon slices.*

The fish soup that forms the focal point of this brunch is a modified version of *cioppino*, the substantial fish stew-soup of San Francisco, created there by immigrant Italian and Portuguese fishermen. That stew customarily contains fish, shellfish, wine, tomatoes, and seasonings. Henry Lewis Creel's recipe calls for non-oily, white-fleshed fish like flounder or sole and clam juice to heighten the flavor. The cook uses either Ricard or Pernod, both anise-based French aperitifs, as a flavor accent.

## WHAT TO DRINK

The fish soup needs a bright, acid white wine; try an Italian Verdicchio or Pinot Grigio or a French Muscadet.

## SHOPPING LIST AND STAPLES

1½ pounds non-oily fish fillets, such as flounder, whitefish, or sole
2 medium-size onions
2 medium-size carrots
2 stalks celery
3 cloves garlic
2 lemons
4 medium-size ripe pears
1 egg
1 cup milk
½ pint heavy cream (optional)
7 tablespoons unsalted butter
16-ounce can Italian plum tomatoes
2 eight-ounce bottles clam juice
2 tablespoons vegetable oil
1 cup yellow cornmeal
1⅓ cups flour
¾ cup sugar
4 teaspoons baking powder
⅛ teaspoon saffron threads, or ¼ teaspoon fennel seeds, or 1 tablespoon paprika
½ teaspoon crushed red pepper
½ teaspoon thyme

80

1 bay leaf
¼ teaspoon cinnamon
¼ teaspoon nutmeg
Salt
½ cup dry white wine
1 tablespoon Ricard or Pernod

## UTENSILS

Large heavy-gauge saucepan with cover
Small saucepan
Muffin pan, preferably cast iron
4 individual ramekins or custard cups
Large bowl
Medium-size bowl
Chef's knife
Paring knife
Wooden spoon
Flour sifter
Citrus juicer (optional)
Zester
Mortar and pestle or rolling pin

## START-TO-FINISH STEPS

**1.** For pear crisp recipe, melt butter in small saucepan and follow steps 1 through 4.
**2.** While pears are baking, using mortar and pestle or rolling pin, separately crush thyme leaves and either saffron threads or fennel seeds, and follow soup recipe steps 1 and 2.
**3.** While soup is simmering, follow muffin recipe steps 1 through 3.
**4.** When pears are done, turn oven up to 400 degrees, and follow muffin recipe step 4.
**5.** Five minutes before muffins are done, follow soup recipe step 3.
**6.** Remove muffins from oven and serve with soup.
**7.** For dessert, follow pear crisp recipe step 5.

## RECIPES

### Fish Soup

3 cloves garlic
2 medium-size onions
2 medium-size carrots
2 stalks celery
2 tablespoons vegetable oil
⅛ teaspoon crushed saffron threads, or ¼ teaspoon crushed fennel seeds, or 1 tablespoon paprika
16-ounce can Italian plum tomatoes
½ cup dry white wine
½ teaspoon crushed red pepper
½ teaspoon crushed thyme leaves
1 bay leaf
2 eight-ounce bottles clam juice
1½ pounds non-oily fish fillets, such as flounder, whitefish or sole, cut into bite-size cubes

1 tablespoon anise-flavored aperitif, such as Ricard or Pernod

**1.** Peel garlic and mince. Peel and chop onions and carrots. Wash, trim, and chop celery. In large heavy-gauge saucepan, heat oil and sauté onions until wilted. Add garlic and cook 1 minute, stirring with wooden spoon.
**2.** Add all other ingredients except fish and aperitif. Bring to a boil, lower heat, and simmer 15 minutes or until vegetables are just tender. Cover to keep warm until serving time.
**3.** When ready to serve, bring soup to a simmer and add fish. Cook 2 to 3 minutes. Watch carefully; the fish cooks quickly. Stir in Ricard or Pernod and serve immediately in warm soup plates or bowls.

### Corn Muffins

5 tablespoons unsalted butter
1 cup yellow cornmeal
1 cup flour
¼ cup sugar
4 teaspoons baking powder
½ teaspoon salt
1 egg
1 cup milk

**1.** Butter 8 muffin cups in cast-iron muffin pan.
**2.** In small saucepan, melt butter.
**3.** Sift dry ingredients into large bowl. Add egg, milk, and melted butter, and, with spoon, stir just until combined.
**4.** Divide batter among muffin cups. Bake in 400-degree oven 20 to 25 minutes.

### Spiced Pear Crisp

½ cup sugar
⅓ cup flour
2 tablespoons unsalted butter, melted
2 tablespoons water
¼ teaspoon cinnamon
¼ teaspoon nutmeg
½ teaspoon grated lemon rind
2 teaspoons lemon juice
4 medium-size ripe pears, peeled, cored, and thinly sliced (about 3 cups)
½ pint heavy cream for garnish (optional)
1 lemon for garnish (optional)

**1.** Preheat oven to 375 degrees. Butter 4 individual ramekins or custard cups.
**2.** In medium-size bowl, combine sugar, flour, melted butter, and water. Using spoon, blend together thoroughly. Mix in cinnamon, nutmeg, lemon rind, and lemon juice.
**3.** Divide pear slices evenly among ramekins.
**4.** Spoon sugar mixture over pear slices and spread mixture to cover fruit. With back of spoon, pat sugar mixture down lightly. Bake 20 to 25 minutes.
**5.** Serve at room temperature. Whip cream, thinly slice lemon, and use as garnish, if desired.

# Bert Greene

B runch is one of my favorite meals. It is the easiest
means of entertaining I know," says New York
cook and author Bert Greene. For a relaxed
brunch, as enjoyable for the cook as for guests,
he recommends casual service and a few light courses.

Trained in French cuisine, Bert Greene is enthusiastic
about American cooking, too; he likes to adapt interna-
tional recipes to indigenous ingredients, creating a "patchwork" cuisine. Brunches should be a patchwork, too, he
believes, and Menu 1 is a perfect example of the Greene
philosophy. With the crêpe main dish, he converts a
French recipe into an American one. Conventional crêpe
batter requires thorough chilling to assure thin, tender
pancakes. In this version, he achieves the same results,
without chilling, by altering the standard ratio of flour and
milk and adding Bloody Mary mix or vegetable juice to
lighten the batter.

In Menu 2, he creates a personal version of a frittata, an
Italian version of the omelet. He adds spaghetti, then
browns the frittata under the broiler. The Parisian pancake (sometimes called Dutch Baby or Plantation Pie) of
Menu 3 resembles a puffy German or Viennese pancake
that is served with brandy, fruit, and confectioners' sugar.
Bert Greene's variation contains cheeses and smoked
meats, resulting in a pancake that is savory rather than
sweet.

*Chilled plum soup, garnished with sour cream and orange zest,
begins this light brunch. Keep extra servings in a glass bowl
over ice. The crêpes, filled with a mixture of seasoned crab
meat, tomato, and cream cheese, are garnished with fresh dill
sprigs. Arrange red onion and avocado slices and watercress
on each plate, or serve the salad on a platter.*

# Plum Soup
# Bloody Mary Crêpes Filled with Crab and Tomatoes
# Avocado and Red Onion Salad

Crêpes, paper-thin French pancakes, look tricky but are not. This cook's crêpes are easy to handle, because they cook through completely without having to be flipped. Use a crêpe pan, if you have one. If not, any well-seasoned or nonstick 7-inch skillet will do. The pan must be hot, and the butter should sizzle but not brown.

To seed and peel tomatoes, drop in boiling water for 30 seconds to loosen the skin. Cool slightly, then peel tomatoes. Cut each tomato in half crosswise, and, holding each half over a bowl, gently squeeze out the seeds.

## WHAT TO DRINK

The piquancy of this meal invites a dry white wine, such as a California Fumé Blanc or an Italian Pinot Grigio.

## SHOPPING LIST AND STAPLES

¾ pound fresh crab meat, preferably, or 2 six-ounce packages frozen king crab meat
2 ripe tomatoes
1 large, ripe avocado
1 stalk fresh rhubarb, preferably, or 16-ounce package frozen
1 orange
2 limes
Watercress sprigs
1 bunch fresh dill
1 medium-size red onion
4 shallots
1 clove garlic
1 egg
¾ cup milk
½ pint heavy cream
1 pint sour cream
2 tablespoons unsalted butter (approximately)
8-ounce package cream cheese
¼ pound Gruyère cheese
16-ounce can purple plums in heavy syrup
6-ounce can Bloody Mary mix or vegetable juice
10½-ounce can bouillon
½ cup olive oil
2 tablespoons vegetable oil
2 teaspoons white wine vinegar
Hot pepper sauce
1 teaspoon Dijon mustard
⅓ cup all-purpose flour
1½ teaspoons cornstarch

1 teaspoon chili powder
¼ teaspoon paprika
¼ teaspoon ground cinnamon
Freshly ground white pepper
Salt and freshly ground pepper
¼ cup dry red wine
2 tablespoons brandy

## UTENSILS

Food processor or blender
Medium-size saucepan
7-inch crêpe pan, preferably nonstick
15½-by-12-inch cookie sheet
Flat plate
Large bowl
Medium-size bowl
2 small bowls
Small cup
Strainer
Measuring cups and spoons
Chef's knife
Paring knife
2 wooden spoons
Plastic cooking spatula (if using nonstick crêpe pan)
Rubber spatula
Whisk
Flour sifter
Cheese grater

## START-TO-FINISH STEPS

*In the morning:* if using frozen crab meat, set out to thaw.

1. Drain and flake crab meat, and follow crêpe recipe step 1. Bring cream cheese to room temperature.
2. If using fresh rhubarb for soup, peel and chop stalk; if using frozen, prepare according to package instructions. Grate and julienne orange zest, and squeeze orange juice.
3. Chop ice, if necessary, for chilling soup. Follow plum soup recipe steps 1 through 3.
4. Juice lime, mince garlic, and prepare avocado and red onion salad, steps 1 through 3.
5. Mince shallots, peel, seed, and chop tomatoes, chop dill, and grate cheese. Lightly butter cookie sheet.
6. Prepare crêpes, steps 2 through 6.
7. While crêpes are heating, follow plum soup recipe step 4.
8. Follow crêpe recipe step 7 and serve with salad.

## Plum Soup

16-ounce can purple plums in heavy syrup
½ cup chopped rhubarb, preferably fresh
¼ cup dry red wine
¼ teaspoon ground cinnamon
¼ teaspoon grated orange peel plus zest for garnish
2 teaspoons orange juice
Dash salt and freshly ground white pepper
1½ teaspoons cornstarch
2 tablespoons brandy
¼ cup heavy cream
½ cup sour cream plus ¼ cup for garnish

1. Drain plums in strainer set over small bowl; reserve syrup. With sharp paring knife, pit plums and place them in medium-size saucepan with reserved syrup, rhubarb, ½ cup water, wine, cinnamon, orange peel, orange juice, salt, and pepper. Bring to a boil and cook 5 minutes.
2. Mix cornstarch and brandy in small cup. Reduce heat under saucepan to medium. In a slow, steady stream, add brandy mixture and cream to the soup. Cook, stirring, until slightly thickened, about 5 minutes.
3. Purée soup in food processor fitted with metal blade or in blender. Turn into serving bowl and place over bowl of chopped ice. Slowly whisk in ½ cup sour cream. Keep over chopped ice until ready to serve, stirring occasionally.
4. Just before serving, stir to combine. Serve in goblets; garnish with sour cream and orange zest.

## Bloody Mary Crêpes Filled with Crab and Tomatoes

*The crêpes:*
¼ cup Bloody Mary mix or vegetable juice
¾ cup milk
1 egg
⅓ cup sifted all-purpose flour
2 tablespoons vegetable oil
Dash salt
¼ teaspoon paprika
1 teaspoon chili powder
Dash hot pepper sauce
2 tablespoons unsalted butter (approximately)

*The filling:*
8-ounce package cream cheese, at room temperature
¾ pound fresh crab meat, preferably, or 2 six-ounce packages frozen king crab meat, thawed, drained, and flaked
4 shallots, minced
2 tablespoons strong bouillon
1 cup sour cream
2 ripe tomatoes, peeled, seeded, and coarsely chopped
½ teaspoon hot pepper sauce
¼ cup chopped fresh dill plus dill sprigs for garnish
¼ cup grated Gruyère cheese

*To make crêpes:*
1. Combine all ingredients for crêpes except butter in food processor or blender. Process 30 seconds. Scrape down sides and process 1 minute more. Pour batter into large bowl and seal with plastic wrap. Let rest at room temperature 30 minutes. The mixture will be quite thick.
2. When ready to make crêpes, stir batter to recombine the mixture. It should be the consistency of heavy cream; if it is too thick, thin it with a little milk. Place paper-towel-lined plate near stove top.
3. Set crêpe pan, preferably with a nonstick surface, over medium heat until hot. Melt 1 tablespoon butter in pan. Holding pan in your left hand, pour in 3 tablespoons of batter. Tilt pan to coat bottom evenly. Set pan back on heat until crêpe starts to bubble, about 30 to 40 seconds. Loosen sides of crêpe with spatula. Invert pan to turn crêpe onto the towel-lined plate. Cover crêpe with another paper towel. Repeat until all the batter is used; add butter to pan as needed.
4. Preheat oven to 350 degrees.

*To make filling:*
5. In medium-size bowl, beat cream cheese with a fork until smooth. Mix in crab meat, shallots, bouillon, sour cream, tomatoes, hot pepper sauce, and chopped dill. Place scant cup of crab filling on each of 4 crêpes, reserving remaining crêpes for later use. Fold the crêpes and place them about 2 inches apart on lightly buttered cookie sheet. Sprinkle with Gruyère.
6. Heat filled crêpes in oven about 15 minutes.
7. Serve crêpes, garnished with fresh dill sprigs.

## Avocado and Red Onion Salad

1 large, ripe avocado
Juice of 1 lime
1 medium-size red onion
Watercress sprigs
1 clove garlic, minced
½ teaspoon salt
1 teaspoon Dijon mustard
2 tablespoons lime juice
2 teaspoons white wine vinegar
½ cup olive oil
Freshly ground pepper

1. Peel avocado and cut into thin slices. Sprinkle with juice of 1 lime.
2. Peel and quarter onion and cut into thin slices. Arrange layers of avocado and onion slices in shallow serving dish. Decorate edges with watercress sprigs.
3. In small bowl, mash garlic and salt to a paste. Stir in remaining ingredients and blend well. Drizzle evenly over salad. Let stand at least 10 minutes before serving.

### LEFTOVER SUGGESTION

Leftover rhubarb, stewed with orange juice and honey, makes a thick sauce that tastes good over lemon sherbet, vanilla ice cream, or pound cake.

# Peasant-Style Frittata
# Asparagus Vinaigrette

*Serve wedges of frittata with asparagus spears on individual trays, and crusty bread, if desired.*

This light brunch welcomes spring with fresh asparagus, cooked, then chilled in a vinaigrette. The peak season for asparagus is April through late June; however, some greengrocers in major cities stock imported asparagus at other times of the year. For the tenderest spears, select those that have plump, nicely rounded stems and compact, pointed tips; wrinkled or thin stems are likely to be tough and stringy. Asparagus perishes rapidly. To keep it fresh, wrap stem ends in dampened paper towels and store in the refrigerator. Peeling the stalks before cooking, as you do for this recipe, usually removes enough of the tough outer flesh to make the entire

spear edible and assures that both tip and stem ends cook uniformly. If you would like to prepare this meal at another season, substitute blanched green beans; canned or frozen asparagus spears are poor substitutes for the fresh.

Pasta, vegetables, ham, and cheese make a savory mixture for the frittata. Assembling this egg dish is simple if you take a few precautions: To keep the spaghetti from clumping when stirred into the beaten eggs, cook it ahead of time, drain, toss with butter or a few drops of oil, and allow it to cool. Cool the sautéed ham and vegetables to room temperature before adding them to the eggs. A hot mixture may scramble them.

## WHAT TO DRINK

First choice here would be either a California Chardonnay or a white French Burgundy. An Italian Chardonnay would be fruitier but equally appropriate.

## SHOPPING LIST AND STAPLES

4 slices cooked ham
2 pounds asparagus of uniform size
Medium-size onion
Medium-size tomato
Small green or red bell pepper
1 lemon
Small bunch parsley (or medium-size bunch, if using for garnish)
Small bunch fresh basil, or 1 teaspoon dried
Small shallot
2 small cloves garlic
3 tablespoons unsalted butter, plus 1 teaspoon (optional)
8 eggs
¼ pound mozzarella cheese
¼ pound Parmesan cheese
¾ cup olive oil
2 teaspoons red wine vinegar
1½ teaspoons Dijon mustard
8-ounce package thin spaghetti
Sugar
½ teaspoon coarse salt
Salt
Freshly ground pepper

## UTENSILS

Food processor (optional)
Large stockpot or kettle with cover
2 large heavy-gauge skillets, 1 with cover
10-inch heavy-gauge skillet with heatproof handle
Large mixing bowl
Small bowl
Colander
Measuring cups and spoons
Chef's knife
Paring knife
2 wooden spoons
2 whisks

Vegetable peeler
Cheese grater (if not using processor)

## START-TO-FINISH STEPS

**1.** Dice ham, chop basil and parsley, and follow frittata recipe steps 1 and 2. While mixture is cooking, follow step 3.
**2.** While spaghetti is cooking, prepare asparagus, steps 1 through 5.
**3.** Using food processor or cheese grater, shred mozzarella and grate Parmesan. Follow frittata recipe steps 4 through 8 and serve frittata with asparagus vinaigrette.

## RECIPES

### Peasant-Style Frittata

Salt
Medium-size onion
Small clove garlic
Medium-size tomato
Small green or red bell pepper
3 tablespoons unsalted butter
    plus 1 teaspoon (optional)
2 teaspoons olive oil
Pinch of sugar
1 teaspoon red wine vinegar
4 slices diced cooked ham (about ½ cup)
2 tablespoons chopped fresh basil, or 1 teaspoon dried
1 tablespoon chopped parsley
20 strands spaghetti
8 eggs
½ cup shredded mozzarella cheese
¼ cup freshly grated Parmesan cheese
¼ teaspoon freshly ground pepper

**1.** In stockpot or kettle, bring 3 quarts of lightly salted hot water to a boil.
**2.** Chop onion, mince garlic, seed and chop tomato, and seed, derib, and chop bell pepper. In large, heavy-gauge skillet, heat 1 tablespoon butter and the oil over medium-low heat. Add onion and garlic, and sauté 2 minutes. Add tomato, bell pepper, sugar, vinegar, and ham. Cook, stirring occasionally, 15 minutes. Add basil and parsley. Stir, remove from heat, and set aside to cool.

**3.** Break spaghetti strands into fourths. Drop pieces into boiling water. Stir once and cook until just tender, about 7 to 8 minutes. Drain in colander. If not adding immediately to egg mixture (step 4), butter very lightly, using about 1 teaspoon butter.

**4.** With whisk, beat eggs with 2 tablespoons cold water in large bowl. Stir in cooled vegetable-and-ham mixture, spaghetti, mozzarella cheese, 2 tablespoons of the Parmesan cheese, and pepper. Mix well. Taste for seasoning.

**5.** Preheat broiler.

**6.** In 10-inch heavy-gauge skillet, heat remaining 2 tablespoons butter over medium heat. When foam subsides, pour in egg mixture. Reduce heat to low and cook, without stirring, about 10 to 12 minutes, or until bottom of frittata is set.

**7.** Sprinkle top with remaining 2 tablespoons Parmesan cheese. Place under broiler until top is set and lightly browned, about 30 to 60 seconds. Watch carefully.

**8.** Cut into pie-shaped wedges and serve.

## Asparagus Vinaigrette

2 pounds asparagus of uniform size
Juice of ½ lemon
Small shallot
Small clove garlic
½ teaspoon coarse salt
1½ teaspoons Dijon mustard
¾ cup olive oil
2 teaspoons red wine vinegar
½ teaspoon freshly ground pepper

**1.** Trim woody ends from asparagus and peel stalks, if desired.

**2.** In large, heavy-gauge skillet, pour water to a depth of ½ inch.

**3.** Lay asparagus in skillet and cook, covered, until tender but still crisp. Cooking time will vary according to size. If spears are thin, start testing at 4 minutes. Thicker spears may require 10 minutes or more. While asparagus are cooking, juice lemon, mince shallot, and crush garlic. Drain asparagus on paper towels. Arrange in shallow serving dish. Sprinkle with shallots.

**4.** In small bowl, mash garlic and salt together with back of spoon until mixture forms a paste. Stir in mustard and lemon juice. Whisk in oil, vinegar, and pepper. Spoon over asparagus.

**5.** Cover and refrigerate asparagus until ready to serve.

---

■■■■■■■■■■

ADDED TOUCH

A very tart lemon ice and the dusky flavor of an espresso coffee coating go well with the main course. (If you are pressed for time, use a store-bought sherbet in place of the homemade lemon ice.) To make perfectly round balls, dip an ice cream scoop into hot water before spooning out the ice. If you prefer a cluster of small balls, use a melon scoop. As a delicious accompaniment to the dessert, serve hot espresso coffee garnished with strips of lemon zest. Be sure to use ground, not instant, espresso.

## Lemon Ice Balls Dusted in Espresso Coffee

1 lemon
1 pint homemade lemon ice (see following recipe), or sherbet
2 teaspoons ground espresso coffee
Fresh mint sprigs for garnish (optional)

**1.** With vegetable peeler, pare 4 strips of rind from lemon. Using an ice cream scoop, press 4 large rounds of lemon ice into 4 individual serving dishes.

**2.** Dust each serving with ½ teaspoon espresso. Keep in freezer until ready to serve.

**3.** Just before serving, garnish each dish with a twist of lemon rind and a mint sprig, if desired.

## Homemade Lemon Ice

6 large lemons
2 cups water
1½ cups sugar

**1.** Using small holes of grater, grate peel of 1 lemon to measure 1 tablespoon. Reserve. With sharp paring knife, remove rind, pith, and seeds from all lemons. Discard. Place pulp in blender or food processor and purée until smooth.

**2.** In small saucepan, combine water and sugar and bring to a boil. Reduce heat and simmer 5 minutes, without stirring. Remove from heat and add lemon purée. Let stand until cool.

**3.** Using the back of a spoon to push it through a coarse-mesh sieve, strain lemon mixture into medium-size bowl. Mix in grated lemon peel and transfer to container of ice cream freezer. Follow manufacturer's directions for freezing.

# Cold Cucumber Soup
# Parisian Pancake
# Pineapple Boat with Hot Sabayon

*The Parisian pancake is served with bowls of cucumber soup. A rich Sabayon sauce accompanies the fruit-filled pineapple boat.*

Chilled cucumber soup, spiked with vodka and flavored with fresh herbs and lemon peel, introduces this nonseasonal brunch. Serve the soup while the pancake bakes. A peeled cucumber is easy to seed: slice in half lengthwise, then in one downward motion, take out the seeds with a melon scoop. For a smooth-textured soup, purée ingredients in a food processor or blender. For a coarser texture, finely mince the cucumber by hand, then combine it with the other ingredients.

The puffed, browned Parisian pancake, resembling an enormous popover, is spectacular when served immediately from the oven. To mix the batter, you can use a food processor or a blender instead of an electric mixer, if you prefer. The recipe for the filling calls for two different smoked meats: turkey and ham. Try to find Black Forest ham, a flavorful variety from Germany. If smoked turkey and ham are unavailable, you can substitute roast turkey and boiled or baked ham.

Pineapples, so named because they resemble giant pinecones, are sweet and juicy only when fully ripe—underripe pineapples are acidic and flavorless. Select a heavy pineapple with a golden yellow rind and dark green crown leaves. The center leaves should pull out easily.

The Sabayon sauce, a French modification of the Italian

egg custard *Zabaglione*, is simple to prepare. Be sure to use a glass or enamel double boiler to cook it; aluminum may discolor the yolks. Beat the sauce constantly with an electric mixer, rotary beater, or whisk. Add the Grand Marnier slowly, or the eggs will not achieve the desired volume. Grand Marnier, a sweet, brandy-based French liqueur, has an intense orange flavor. Curaçao, or any other orange-flavored liqueur, is an acceptable substitute.

## WHAT TO DRINK

This menu sets out warm, familiar flavors very simply and directly. Serve a young, fruity California Zinfandel, a Beaujolais, or a good Chianti Classico—not a Riserva.

## SHOPPING LIST AND STAPLES

¼ pound sliced smoked ham, preferably Black Forest
¼ pound sliced smoked turkey
2 medium-size cucumbers
Small bunch scallions
Small bunch fresh parsley
Small bunch fresh basil, or 2 teaspoons dried
Small bunch fresh mint
1 shallot
1 medium-size pineapple
1 orange
1 lemon
1 kiwi (optional)
1 pint fresh strawberries
Small bunch grapes (optional)
6 tablespoons unsalted butter
7 eggs
1 cup milk
3 cups plain yogurt
¼ pound mozzarella cheese
¼ pound Parmesan cheese
1½ cups chicken stock, preferably homemade (see page 13), or canned
1 cup flour
¼ cup sugar
Red pepper flakes
Salt and freshly ground black pepper
Freshly ground white pepper
¼ cup vodka
3 tablespoons Grand Marnier, or other orange liqueur
2 tablespoons Madeira

## UTENSILS

Food processor or blender
Medium-size heavy-gauge saucepan
10-inch cast-iron skillet
Double boiler
2 large bowls
Measuring cups and spoons
Chef's knife
Paring knife
Wooden spoons
Rubber spatula
Vegetable peeler
Grapefruit knife
Citrus grater
Cheese grater
Electric mixer

## START-TO-FINISH STEPS

**1.** Chill soup bowls. For cucumber soup, chop parsley, basil, and mint, and grate lemon peel.
**2.** Follow soup recipe step 1.
**3.** While soup is cooking, follow pancake recipe steps 1 and 2.
**4.** Follow soup recipe step 2.
**5.** For pancake recipe, cube mozzarella, grate Parmesan, and follow steps 3 through 5.
**6.** While pancake is baking, separate remaining 3 eggs and refrigerate whites for another use. Then follow pineapple recipe steps 1 through 3.
**7.** About 15 minutes before pancake is finished baking, remove soup from refrigerator and serve.
**8.** Remove pancake from oven and serve.
**9.** For dessert, follow pineapple recipe step 4.

## RECIPES

### Cold Cucumber Soup

2 medium-size cucumbers
3 scallions
1½ cups chicken stock
2 tablespoons chopped fresh parsley
2 tablespoons chopped fresh basil, or 2 teaspoons dried
1 tablespoon chopped fresh mint
1 teaspoon grated lemon peel

90

3 cups plain yogurt
¼ cup vodka
Salt and freshly ground white pepper

1. Peel, seed, and chop cucumbers and clean and chop 2 scallions. In medium-size saucepan, combine cucumber, chopped scallions, stock, parsley, basil, mint, and lemon peel. Bring to a boil and cook 10 minutes. Clean remaining scallion and shred green. Remove soup from heat and place over large bowl of ice to hasten cooling.
2. In food processor fitted with metal blade or in blender, purée cucumber mixture until smooth. Stir in yogurt and vodka. Add salt and pepper to taste. Place in chilled serving bowls and garnish with scallion shreds. Keep chilled until ready to serve.

## Parisian Pancake

4 eggs
1 cup all-purpose flour
1 cup milk
1 shallot
¼ pound sliced smoked ham, preferably Black Forest
¼ pound sliced smoked turkey
6 tablespoons butter
2 tablespoons Madeira
Salt and freshly ground black pepper
Pinch of red pepper flakes
¾ cup cubed mozzarella cheese
¼ cup freshly grated Parmesan cheese

1. Preheat oven to 425 degrees.
2. Place eggs, flour, and milk in large mixing bowl and, using electric mixer, beat until smooth. Scrape down sides of bowl and beat again briefly. Or, in large bowl, beat with electric mixer. Chill batter in freezer until needed.
3. Mince shallot and chop ham and turkey. Melt 2 tablespoons butter in 10-inch cast-iron skillet. Sauté shallots until golden. Add ham and Madeira. Cook over medium heat until all liquid is absorbed. Stir in turkey, salt and pepper to taste, and red pepper flakes.
4. Dot surface with remaining 4 tablespoons butter. Place in oven briefly, just until bubbly.
5. Meanwhile, remove batter from freezer and briefly process or beat to recombine. Remove skillet from oven. Sprinkle mozzarella cheese over ham and turkey. Pour batter over top and sprinkle with Parmesan cheese. Bake 25 minutes. Remove from oven and serve immediately.

## Pineapple Boat with Hot Sabayon

1 medium-size pineapple
1 kiwi (optional)
1 cup fresh strawberries
3 egg yolks
¼ cup sugar
¼ cup orange juice
3 tablespoons Grand Marnier, or other orange liqueur
1 teaspoon grated orange peel (optional)
Small bunch grapes (optional)

1. With leaves attached, cut pineapple in half lengthwise. Cut around flesh with a grapefruit knife; remove flesh, leaving shell intact. (Reserve other half and use for another meal.) Cut flesh into bite-size pieces.
2. If using, peel and slice kiwi. Rinse strawberries briefly in cool water, then halve them. Combine with pineapple pieces and kiwi, if using. Fill pineapple shell with fruit and refrigerate, loosely covered.
3. Combine egg yolks, sugar, orange juice, and 2 tablespoons liqueur in top of double boiler over simmering water (top of double boiler should not touch water). Beat mixture with electric mixer 4 to 5 minutes, until consistency is that of lightly whipped cream. Blend in remaining liqueur. Transfer to serving dish and sprinkle with orange peel, if desired.
4. Serve lukewarm or at room temperature with the chilled fruit. Garnish with grapes, if desired.

*1. Crack egg against side of bowl.*

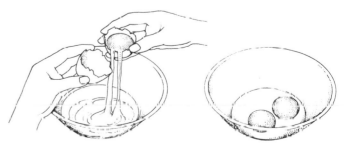

*2. Separate each egg by pouring back and forth between halves of shell until the entire white has dropped into one bowl.*

# Shelley Handler

MENU 1 (Left)
**Buckwheat Cakes**
**Spiced Cranberries and Pears**
**Whipped Cream with Maple Syrup**
**Pan-Fried Ham Steaks**
**Gingered Apples**

MENU 2
**Pears with Gorgonzola and Walnuts**
**Italian Sausages**
**Fennel and Red-Pepper Sauté**

MENU 3
**Smoked Salmon and Black Caviar**
**Soft-Boiled Eggs with Asparagus Spears and Toast**
**Scones with "Melted" Strawberries**
**and Crème Fraîche**

Shelley Handler, a professional chef and cooking instructor, considers cooking an art form, no less serious than painting or sculpture. She likes to begin her mornings with a stroll through the produce markets of San Francisco's Chinatown, where fresh produce is artfully and colorfully arranged. The aesthetics of cooked food matter as much to her. "One eats first with the eyes, so I take care with the colors and textures of a meal," she says.

Because she lived and worked in Italy, many of her recipes are influenced by Italian cooking, but she prefers spicy, full-flavored foods whatever their country of origin. In Menu 1, Shelley Handler uses distinctive, nutty buckwheat flour. Other assertive flavors come from the spiced cranberry and pear relish and from the smoky ham. All three courses of Menu 2 feature strong Italian flavors: pears with Gorgonzola, fennel sausages, and fennel sautéed with red pepper and onion. In Menu 3, smoked salmon and caviar accent the boiled eggs and scones.

*Spiced cranberry and pear sauce, garnished here with orange zest, tops the stack of buckwheat pancakes. Serve the pan-fried ham steak and the gingered apples on the same plate and pass the maple-flavored whipped cream in a separate dish.*

# Buckwheat Cakes
## Spiced Cranberries and Pears / Whipped Cream with Maple Syrup
## Pan-Fried Ham Steaks / Gingered Apples

**B**uckwheat cakes have been a winter morning treat in America for over a century. The bittersweet, nutty buckwheat flour often is combined with an unbleached white flour, as in this recipe, to temper the strong buckwheat taste. The batter combines more readily if the dry and wet ingredients are mixed separately before being blended together. Stir the batter until it is just smooth. Too much stirring yields tough pancakes.

The smokey flavor of ham is a delicious contrast to the gingered apples served on the side. Fresh ginger root is a main seasoning for the apples. Available in most well-stocked supermarkets and greengrocers, fresh ginger should be firm and smooth, its skin pale tan. Avoid ginger that is shriveled or soft.

## WHAT TO DRINK

The interplay of flavors in this menu requires a dry, full-bodied white wine, such as a California Chardonnay or an Alsatian Gewürztraminer.

## SHOPPING LIST AND STAPLES

4 slices center-cut ham, each about ⅓ pound in weight
  and ⅓ inch thick
4 medium-size firm apples, such as Red Delicious or
  McIntosh
Small piece fresh ginger
¼ pound unpackaged fresh cranberries, or 12-ounce bag
Small pear, preferably Bosc or Comice
Small orange
1 lemon
1 stick unsalted butter (approximately)
¾ cup milk
½ pint heavy cream
1 egg
½ pint apple cider, preferably unpasteurized
Pure maple syrup
½ cup buckwheat flour
½ cup unbleached white flour
2 teaspoons baking powder
½ cup plus ½ teaspoon sugar (approximately)
3½ tablespoons chopped almonds or pecans
¼ teaspoon ground cinnamon
Cinnamon stick
5 coriander seeds
2 whole cloves
Salt

## UTENSILS

Griddle or large cast-iron skillet
Large cast-iron skillet with cover
Medium-size heavy-gauge saucepan with cover
Small saucepan
Large heavy-gauge sauté pan or skillet with cover
Large bowl
2 medium-size bowls
Colander
Measuring cups and spoons
Chef's knife
Paring knife
2 wooden spoons
Ladle or large spoon
Large spatula
Rubber spatula
Wire whisk
Citrus juicer (optional)
Grater
Flour sifter
Electric mixer

## START-TO-FINISH STEPS

**1.** Follow buckwheat cakes recipe steps 1 through 3.

**2.** While batter is resting, follow cranberries recipe step 1. Preheat oven to 350 degrees.

**3.** As syrup for cranberries cooks, grate orange peel and, if desired, cut julienne strips of zest.

**4.** Follow cranberries recipe steps 2 and 3. Chill medium-size bowl and beaters for whipping cream. For whipped cream recipe, toast nuts on baking sheet in preheated oven 5 to 10 minutes, or until light brown. Shake nuts occasionally and watch carefully to keep from scorching.

**5.** Follow cranberries recipe step 4.

**6.** While nuts are toasting and cranberries are cooking, follow gingered apples recipe steps 1 through 4.

**7.** Remove nuts from oven and allow to cool. Lower oven temperature to 200 degrees. Follow cranberries recipe step 5.

**8.** As cranberries cool, follow gingered apples recipe steps 5 through 7.

**9.** Follow ham steaks recipe steps 1 and 2.

**10.** Follow buckwheat cakes recipe steps 4 and 5.

**11.** While you are making the buckwheat cakes, follow whipped cream recipe steps 1 and 2.

**12.** Follow ham steaks recipe step 3, buckwheat cakes recipe step 6, and serve.

# RECIPES

## Buckwheat Cakes

5 tablespoons unsalted butter (approximately)
¾ cup milk, at room temperature
1 egg
1 tablespoon pure maple syrup
½ cup buckwheat flour
½ cup unbleached white flour
2 teaspoons baking powder
½ teaspoon salt
Spiced cranberries and pears (see following recipe)
Julienne strips of orange zest (optional)
Whipped cream with maple syrup (see following recipe)

**1.** In small saucepan, melt 2½ tablespoons butter. Put milk, egg, maple syrup, and melted butter in large bowl. With wooden spoon, stir just until ingredients are combined.
**2.** In medium-size bowl, sift together the 2 flours, baking powder, and salt.
**3.** Add dry ingredients to milk and egg mixture. Whisk just until flour is moistened. Be careful not to overbeat. Cover and let batter rest at least 20 minutes, or until ready to use.
**4.** With ½ teaspoon or so of butter, grease griddle or large cast-iron skillet. Heat over medium-high heat until a drop of cold water evaporates on contact. Holding ladle or large spoon close to griddle to better control shape of pancake, pour in 2 to 3 tablespoons batter. After 1 minute or so, using large spatula, check bottom of pancake and, when nicely browned, turn.
**5.** When second side has browned, transfer pancake to ovenproof platter and keep warm in oven. Put plates in oven to warm. Continue making pancakes, adding butter to griddle as needed.
**6.** Remove plates and buckwheat cakes from oven. Divide pancakes among warm plates. Top with cranberries and garnish with orange zest, if desired. Serve with ham and apples, and bowl of whipped cream.

## Spiced Cranberries and Pears

½ cup sugar
¼ cup lemon juice
¾ cup water
1 cinnamon stick
5 coriander seeds
2 whole cloves
¼ pound fresh cranberries (about 1 cup)
Small pear
½ teaspoon grated orange rind

**1.** In medium-size heavy-gauge saucepan, combine sugar, lemon juice, water, cinnamon stick, coriander seeds, and cloves. Bring to a boil, then cook over medium heat 5 minutes.
**2.** In colander, briefly rinse cranberries; drain. Remove any stems and damaged berries.
**3.** Peel and core pear. Cut into small pieces. Add pear to syrup and cook, covered, another 5 minutes.
**4.** Add cranberries to syrup and cook until berries pop and syrup thickens, about 10 minutes.
**5.** Remove from heat and let cool 10 minutes. Stir in grated orange rind.

## Whipped Cream with Maple Syrup

½ pint heavy cream, chilled
1 tablespoon pure maple syrup
3½ tablespoons finely chopped toasted almonds or pecans

**1.** In chilled medium-size bowl, lightly whip cream with an electric mixer. Add maple syrup. Whip until cream stands in peaks.
**2.** With rubber spatula, fold in chopped nuts, reserving a few for garnish. Turn whipped cream into serving bowl and sprinkle with reserved nuts.

## Pan-Fried Ham Steaks

4 slices center-cut ham steaks, each about ⅓ pound in weight and ⅓ inch thick

**1.** Trim fat from ham; melt fat in large cast-iron skillet.
**2.** Cook ham steaks over medium heat, turning once, until edges begin to curl and ham is slightly browned, about 10 minutes. Cover and keep warm until ready to serve.
**3.** Just before serving, drain on paper towels.

## Gingered Apples

Small piece fresh ginger
4 medium-size firm apples
3 tablespoons butter
¼ teaspoon ground cinnamon
6 tablespoons apple cider
½ teaspoon sugar (approximately)
Pinch of salt

**1.** Peel ginger and grate on smallest holes of grater.
**2.** Peel, core, halve, and slice apples into ¼-inch-thick crescents.
**3.** In large heavy-gauge sauté pan or skillet, melt 2 tablespoons butter. Add apple slices and sauté over moderate heat 2 minutes, turning once.
**4.** Sprinkle in ginger and cinnamon, and mix well; toss gently to blend with apples. Sauté about 1 minute, turning once.
**5.** Add cider, sugar, and salt. Taste for seasoning and sweetness; adjust if necessary.
**6.** Cut remaining tablespoon butter into small bits and set aside. Cook apples until barely tender and sauce is slightly thickened, about 2 minutes. Raise heat to further reduce sauce if necessary. During last minute of cooking, stir in cut-up tablespoon butter to sauce.
**7.** Cover and keep warm off heat until ready to serve.

# Pears with Gorgonzola and Walnuts
# Italian Sausages
# Fennel and Red-Pepper Sauté

*This informal fall brunch features Italian sausages, sautéed fennel and red pepper, and pears filled with creamy Gorgonzola.*

Pears stuffed with Gorgonzola are a dramatic fruit course in this Italian-style brunch. As an alternate for the Gorgonzola, an Italian blue cheese, Shelley Handler suggests using "Torta di Mascarpone e Gorgonzola," a layered cake of two cheeses imported from Italy. Creamy, rich mascarpone is produced in limited quantities in the fall. Its mild taste is a delightful foil for the sharpness of Gorgonzola.

The licorice flavor of fennel, a vegetable that resembles celery, is dominant in both of the other two dishes. Fennel sausages are sold in Italian groceries, but if you cannot find them, use Italian sweet sausages instead. Blanched fennel is one of the components of the vegetable dish.

## WHAT TO DRINK

Since the flavor of fennel is prominent in this menu, a young, fruity red wine would be best. First choice would be a Chianti Classico, but a French Beaujolais or California Gamay would also do well.

## SHOPPING LIST AND STAPLES

4 to 8 home-style Italian sausages (about 1 to 1½ pounds total weight), preferably with fennel, or good-quality sweet sausages
2 medium-size or 3 small fennel bulbs

1 red bell pepper
Small red onion
2 large ripe pears, preferably Comice or Bosc
1 lemon
6 tablespoons unsalted butter (approximately)
1 tablespoon heavy cream or cream cheese
½ cup walnut halves
¼ pound Gorgonzola
2 tablespoons olive oil
Salt
¼ cup dry white wine

## UTENSILS

2 large heavy-gauge skillets or sauté pans
Medium-size saucepan
Ovenproof baking dish
13-by-9-by-2-inch baking sheet
Small bowl
Colander
Measuring cups and spoons
Chef's knife
Paring knife
Wooden spoon
Spatula
Rolling pin

## START-TO-FINISH STEPS

1. Follow pears recipe steps 1 and 2.
2. While walnuts are toasting, follow fennel recipe steps 1 through 3.
3. Remove walnuts from oven and allow to cool.
4. Follow fennel recipe step 4, pears recipe steps 3 and 4, and sausages recipe step 1.
5. Follow pears recipe steps 5 and 6, and serve.
6. Follow sausages recipe step 2, fennel recipe step 5, and serve.

## RECIPES

### Pears with Gorgonzola and Walnuts

½ cup walnut halves
¼ pound Gorgonzola
3 to 4 tablespoons unsalted butter, at room temperature
1 tablespoon heavy cream or cream cheese
2 large ripe pears
1 lemon, halved

1. Preheat oven to 350 degrees.
2. Spread walnut halves on baking sheet and toast in oven 5 to 8 minutes, or until golden brown. Watch carefully to make sure they do not burn.
3. In small bowl, blend Gorgonzola, butter, and heavy cream or cream cheese.
4. With rolling pin, crush walnuts between pieces of wax paper. Add scant ¼ cup nuts to cheese and mix well.
5. Wash pears well and pat dry with paper towels. Peel, if desired. Slice pears in half lengthwise, and remove cores. Slice thin piece off rounded side of each half so it will lie flat. Rub pears with lemon to prevent discoloration.
6. Stuff pear halves with cheese mixture. Sprinkle remaining nuts over each half. Arrange on individual plates.

### Italian Sausages

4 to 8 home-style Italian sausages
¼ cup dry white wine

1. Prick sausages, place in ovenproof baking dish, and add wine. Cover dish with aluminum foil and bake 20 minutes at 350 degrees. Remove from oven and set aside.
2. In large heavy-gauge skillet or sauté pan, cook sausages, about 5 to 7 minutes, turning occasionally with spatula to make sure they brown evenly. Do not overcook.

### Fennel and Red-Pepper Sauté

2 medium-size or 3 small fennel bulbs
1 red bell pepper
½ small red onion
2 tablespoons olive oil
2 tablespoons butter
Salt

1. In medium-size saucepan, bring 2 cups water to a boil.
2. Trim fennel, cutting away stems at bulb. Cut bulb in half lengthwise. Cut out core and remove any tough or blemished outer layers. Cut lengthwise into thin strips.
3. Drop fennel into boiling water and cook about 3 minutes. Drain in colander.
4. Core, seed, and derib bell pepper; slice thinly. Peel red onion, slice, and separate into rings.
5. In large heavy-gauge skillet or sauté pan, heat olive oil and butter. Add red pepper and onion, and sauté until tender, about 1 minute. Add fennel and continue to sauté until tender-crisp, about 3 minutes. Season with scant pinch of salt.

# Smoked Salmon and Black Caviar
# Soft-Boiled Eggs with Asparagus Spears and Toast
# Scones with "Melted" Strawberries and Crème Fraîche

*Arrange the asparagus spears, toast triangles, and salmon with caviar around the soft-boiled egg in its cup. On a separate plate, offer the split scones with a ladleful of strawberries and a dollop of crème fraîche or whipped cream.*

Smoked salmon served with caviar is an elegant component of this light spring brunch. Mild, lightly salted Scandinavian or Pacific Northwest smoked salmon tastes better here than lox, a salt-cured salmon. Ask your supplier to slice the salmon paper thin. Imported caviars, like black Russian Beluga or Sevruga, are luxury foods. However, moderately priced red saltwater salmon or golden whitefish caviar work perfectly well in this recipe.

Scones are sweet Scottish breads similar to Southern biscuits. The accompanying "melted" strawberries are really a compote—the berries remain whole after heating. But here, you use them as a jam. When you buy strawberries, select a container with no red stains; stains are a sign that the berries may be old. Check that the berries at the bottom are not under- or overripe. To wash strawberries, immerse them in cold water for 30 seconds, rinse under running water, and drain thoroughly. You can serve the scones whole, topped with strawberries and crème fraîche, like a strawberry shortcake; or you can split them open, spread them with jam and crème fraîche, and eat them like biscuits.

## WHAT TO DRINK

To complement the asparagus, choose a non-vintage French Champagne or a good-quality sparkling wine.

## SHOPPING LIST AND STAPLES

6 ounces thinly sliced smoked salmon
20 spears slender young asparagus (about 1½ pounds total weight)
1 head chicory
Small red onion
2 pints strawberries
Small lemon, plus 1 additional (optional)
1 stick unsalted butter
7 eggs
1 pint heavy cream, or ½ pint if using commercial crème fraîche
1 cup crème fraîche, preferably homemade (see page 9), or commercial (optional)
2-ounce jar black or golden caviar
8 thin slices whole-grain wheat or rye bread
2 cups flour
3 teaspoons baking powder
¼ cup plus 2 tablespoons sugar (approximately)
Salt

## UTENSILS

Large enamel skillet
2 medium-size saucepans
15½-by-12-inch cookie sheet
Large mixing bowl
Small mixing bowl
Small cup
Colander
Measuring cups and spoons
Chef's knife
Paring knife
Slotted spoon or wire skimmer
2 wooden spoons
Grater
Wire whisk
Flour sifter
Pastry blender
Pastry brush
Vegetable peeler (optional)
Toaster
Salad spinner (optional)

## START-TO-FINISH STEPS

*In the morning:* If you would like to make quick crème fraîche, combine 1 cup heavy cream and 1 tablespoon lemon juice in screwtop jar. Mix well, cover, and let stand at room temperature until thick, about 4 hours. For regular crème fraîche, see recipe on page 9.

1. Grate lemon rind and follow strawberries recipe steps 1 and 2.
2. Prepare eggs with asparagus, step 1.
3. Follow scones recipe steps 1 through 4. Cover loosely with kitchen towel.
4. Follow smoked salmon recipe steps 1 and 2. Chill bowl and beaters if serving scones with whipped cream.
5. Follow eggs with asparagus recipe steps 2 and 3. If using whipped cream for scones, whip cream and refrigerate while eggs and asparagus are cooking.
6. Uncover scones and follow step 5.
7. Follow eggs with asparagus recipe steps 4 through 6.
8. Follow scones recipe step 6. Cover and refrigerate until ready to serve.
9. Place egg cups in centers of plates with salmon rolls. Arrange asparagus spears and toast triangles around

cups. Carefully remove tops of eggshells. (Asparagus and toast are to be dipped into warm egg yolk.) Serve as main course.

**10.** If using whipped cream, remove from refrigerator and stir once or twice with whisk. Then follow scones recipe step 7, and serve for dessert.

---

## RECIPES

### Smoked Salmon and Black Caviar

Small red onion
½ head chicory
6 ounces thinly sliced smoked salmon
2-ounce jar black or golden caviar
Lemon slices for garnish (optional)

**1.** Peel onion and slice thinly.
**2.** Wash chicory and dry in salad spinner or pat dry with paper towels. Separate leaves and form bed on side of each plate. Top with rolled-up smoked salmon slices and red onion slices. Spoon caviar over smoked salmon and garnish with lemon slices, if desired. Cover loosely and set aside until ready to serve.

### Soft-Boiled Eggs with Asparagus Spears and Toast

20 spears slender young asparagus (about 1½ pounds
  total weight)
4 eggs
8 thin slices whole-grain wheat or rye
  bread, toasted

**1.** Prepare asparagus: bend stems and snap where natural breaks occur, an inch or so from ends. Or you may peel the stems, trimming away woody ends.
**2.** In medium-size saucepan, bring 1 quart water to a boil. Gently add eggs to saucepan and boil 4 minutes.
**3.** In large enamel skillet, bring 3 to 4 cups water to a boil. Add asparagus, a few stalks at a time, to skillet. Maintain vigorous boil. Cook asparagus until *al dente* and bright green, 4 to 10 minutes, depending on thickness of stems. Be careful not to overcook.
**4.** While asparagus is cooking, toast bread and cut in half diagonally.
**5.** Quickly remove asparagus with slotted spoon or large skimmer. Drain in colander.
**6.** Remove eggs and transfer to egg cups.

### Scones with "Melted" Strawberries and Crème Fraîche

2 cups flour
3 teaspoons baking powder
½ teaspoon salt
5 tablespoons well-chilled butter
3 eggs
½ cup heavy cream (approximately)
2 tablespoons sugar (approximately)
"Melted" strawberries (see following recipe)
Crème fraîche or whipped cream

**1.** Preheat oven to 425 degrees.
**2.** In large bowl, sift together flour, baking powder, and salt. With pastry blender or 2 knives, cut in chilled butter until mixture is crumbly.
**3.** In small mixing bowl, lightly beat 2 eggs with ½ cup cream. Make a well in flour mixture and add eggs and cream. Stir gently just until liquid is incorporated. If more liquid is necessary, add more cream. Dough should be soft and moist but hold its shape.
**4.** Turn out dough onto lightly floured surface and knead 15 times. Cut dough into fourths and form each piece into a ball. Place well apart on buttered cookie sheet and tap down into ½-inch-thick rounds. Cut each round into quarters, without cutting all the way through.
**5.** In small cup, beat 1 egg with 1 tablespoon water. Brush scones with egg wash and sprinkle with sugar.
**6.** Bake 10 to 15 minutes or until golden brown. Remove from oven and cover with kitchen towel to keep warm.
**7.** Transfer scones to serving plates. Split open and top with berries and crème fraîche or whipped cream.

### "Melted" Strawberries

2 pints strawberries
¼ cup sugar
½ teaspoon grated lemon rind

**1.** In colander, briefly rinse strawberries; drain and gently pat dry with paper towels. Hull and halve strawberries.
**2.** In medium-size saucepan, combine strawberries and sugar. Cook over medium-low heat 5 minutes, stirring occasionally. Add grated lemon rind. The berries should be soft and syrupy. If consistency is too thin, remove berries with slotted spoon, increase heat, and reduce liquid until thick and syrupy. Remove pan from heat. Return berries to syrup and let cool.

# Acknowledgments

The Editors particularly wish to thank the following for their contributions to the conception and production of these books: Ezra Bowen, Judith Brennan, Angelica Cannon, Elizabeth Schneider Colchie, Sally Dorst, Florence Fabricant, Marion Flynn, Lilyan Glusker, Frieda Henry, Jay Jacobs, Pearl Lau, Kim MacArthur, Kay Noble, Elizabeth Noll, Fran Shinagel, Martha Tippin, Ann Topper, Jack Ubaldi, Joan Whitman.

The Editors would also like to thank the following for their courtesy in lending items for photography: *Cover:* cloth—Brunschwig and Fils; platters—Eigen Arts Pottery; flatware—Wallace Silversmiths. *Frontispiece:* bowl, basket—Pottery Barn; pitcher, glasses, coffee pot, mugs—Dean & DeLuca. *Pages 18–19:* cloth—Ad Hoc Software; front basket—F. O. Merz; remaining baskets—Be Seated; napkins, dishes, pitcher, flatware—Wolfman, Gold & Good Co. *Pages 22–23:* dishes—Metlox; flatware—Wallace Silversmiths. *Page 25:* countertop—Formica® Brand Laminate by Formica Corp.; mat, napkin, plate, flatware—Henri Bendel. *Pages 28–29:* glasses, plates—Spode, Inc.; glass bowl—The Pilgrim Glass Corp.; flatware—Wallace Silversmiths. *Pages 32–33:* cloth— Primitive Artisans; napkins—Leacock and Company; glass plates—Glazer Sales; white plates—Buffalo China, Inc.; flatware, trays—Pottery Barn. *Page 35:* cloth—Fabindia from Primitive Artisans; dishes—Conran's; flatware—Wallace Silversmiths. *Pages 38–39:* cloth—Pierre Deux; blue plates, glass bowl—Dean & DeLuca; beige plates—Laura Ashley. *Page 42:* cloth, napkins, dishes, coffee pot—Pierre Deux; vases—Pottery Barn; flatware—Wallace Silversmiths. *Page 45:* cloth—Brunschwig and Fils; bowls—Williams-Sonoma; plate—Buffalo China, Inc.; flatware—Wallace Silversmiths. *Pages 48–49:* napkins—Fabindia from Primitive Artisans; bowl, vase—The Pilgrim Glass Corp., plates—Williams-Sonoma. *Pages 52–53:* napkins—Fabrications; plates—Pottery Barn; flatware—The Lauffer Company. *Page 55:* cloth, napkins, flatware—Williams-Sonoma; dishes—Pottery Barn. *Page 62:* mat—Fabrications; dishes—Pottery Barn; flatware—The Lauffer Company. *Page 64:* hand-painted cloth—Peter Fasano; plate—Fiesta. *Pages 66–67:* trays, dishes—Mitsukoshi; flatware—The Lauffer Company. *Page 70:* napkins—Conran's; dishes—Museum of American Art Folk Shop. *Page 72:* plates, glasses—Cue Group. *Pages 74–75:* cloth, napkin—New Country Gear; pots—The Pilgrim Glass Corp.; dishes, underplates, picture—Soovia Janis; flatware—The Lauffer Company. *Page 78:* mat, bowl—Henri Bendel; napkins—Conran's; flatware, plate—Wolfman, Gold & Good Co.; *Page 79:* mat, small bowl, flatware—Wolfman, Gold & Good Co.; soup bowl, plate—Buffalo China, Inc. *Pages 82–83:* mat, napkin, flatware, plate—Henri Bendel; hand-painted cloth—Peter Fasano; saucer—Metlox. *Page 86:* mat, basket, dishes—Folklorica Imports, Inc.; flatware—Henri Bendel. *Page 89:* countertop—Formica® Brand Laminate by Formica Corp.; platter, bowl—Terrafirma; baskets, flatware—Folklorica Imports, Inc., *Pages 92–93:* hand-woven mat—Museum of American Folk Art Shop; napkin—Fabindia from Primitive Artisans; dish—Buffalo China, Inc. *Page 96:* dishes—George Briard Folk Ways; mug—Pottery Barn; flatware—Wallace Silversmiths. *Page 98:* napkin—D. Porthault, Inc.; flatware—Wallace Silversmiths. *Kitchen equipment courtesy of:* White-Westinghouse, Commercial Aluminum Cookware Co., Robot-Coupe, Caloric, Hobart Corp.

Illustrations by Ray Skibinski
Production by Giga Communications

# Index

*Time-Life Books Inc. offers a wide range of fine recordings, including a Big Band series. For subscription information, call 1-800-621-7026, or write TIME-LIFE MUSIC, Time & Life Building, Chicago, Illinois 60611.*